"A House Divided..."

✦ ✦ ✦

A Century of Great Civil War Quotations

✦ ✦ ✦

Edited by Edward L. Ayers
Researched and Compiled by Kate Cohen

Produced by Amaranth

John Wiley & Sons, Inc.
New York • Chichester • Weinheim • Brisbane • Singapore • Toronto

Contents

✯ ✯ ✯

Introduction

The people in this book speak directly to us. We hear the voice of command and the voice of the common soldier. We hear those who speak without hope and others who hope even when they have every reason to give up. We hear the weariness of older people and the confusion of the young. We hear the voice of sympathy across the battle lines and the voice of vengeance and hatred. We hear the resignation of the wounded and the despair of those who survive. We hear the pride of victorious generals and the crushing doubt of those who sacrificed lives in a losing cause. Some of the words have become famous while others have passed from our collective memory.

We have organized this book so that we can follow these complicated conversations more easily. The topics range from the battlefield to the homefront, from the hospital tent to the prison cell, from New England to Texas. Men and women, black and white, soldier and civilian, all get their say. Secessionists and Unionists, heroes and deserters, warriors and peacemakers speak their minds.

The chapters also follow a chronological sequence. People chose different words as the years unfolded, as they saw more of what this war meant. The cockiness of 1860 rapidly became the fury of 1861, the horror of 1862, the wild determination of 1863, the resoluteness of 1864, and the mingled sadness and relief of 1865.

A book of quotations such as this one, juxtaposing words and phrases across battle lines and across years, shows the importance of words themselves. The words stand not merely as vehicles of emotion, but define and evoke emotions. Just as the open battlefields of First Manassas became replaced with the trenches of Cold Harbor, muskets with rifles, and volunteers with conscripts, so did some words displace others. Early in the conflict, words such as *decisive, glory, brilliant,* and *gallant* punctuated the hopeful pronouncements and predictions of both sides. As the war unfolded, people spoke more of *vengeance, subjugation,* and *humiliation.* They mixed images of *peace* with images of *extermination* and *devastation,* sometimes in the same letter. Anything that would end the killing.

Northerners and Southerners, we see, often used identical words to express their deepest motives and emotions. Words such as *God* and *Christian* grace the diaries, letters, and editorials of those on both sides. Both felt certain that their side bore the highest divine sanction. They habitually linked the spiritual and the secular, calling their causes and their sacrifices *righteous* and *sacred.*

Both Union and Confederate soldiers also spoke repeatedly, ritualistically, of *duty, country, liberty, patriotism,* and *honor.* Both sides invoked *courage* and *blood, manliness* and *nobility* at every opportunity. All these words people knew to be the language of warfare, the language they had learned from the Bible, their history books, and the speeches they heard on election day. They instinctually turned to this stirring rhetoric when lesser words seemed pale and inadequate.

Despite the language they shared, however, those in the Union and those in the Confederacy also chose words they deemed especially suited to their cause. Northerners rallied to the call of *Union* and *Constitution;* identifying their enemies as *traitors, rebels,* and *aristocrats,* their opponents' actions as *rebellion* and *crime.* Those above the Mason-Dixon line saw themselves as fighting for order and the rule of law, for the peaceful transfer of power through open elections. They pictured themselves as the heirs to the nation created by the Founding Fathers.

Southerners, for their part, pictured themselves as the heirs of the Revolution itself, of the struggle for independence. In their eyes, the nation was not as important as the principles for which they thought it stood; the nation was merely a vehicle for their freedom. The key words in the Confederate lexicon leaped from the Revolutionary struggle. Southerners saw themselves as *patriots* fighting for *independence* from the *unconstitutional aggression* and *invasion* of a *tyrannical* and arrogant central government, just as their forefathers had three generations earlier. They were proud to call themselves *rebels,* though in their eyes there was nothing of treason involved in their actions. The considered themselves rebels just as George Washington had been a rebel.

Confederates thought that Northerners had usurped the federal government for their own selfish ends, violating the spirit of the Constitution on which the states had agreed. Southerners, whether they thought it was wise or not, believed that they had the right to leave the Union if they so chose. And when they did, they became, in their own eyes, *defenders* of their *independence* and *pride* from the *submission* and *slavery* the North would inflict upon them. Northerners at the time and many people ever since have refused to accept the sincerity of white Southerners who could use such words when they themselves were a slaveholding people. Even though most white Southern families did not themselves own slaves, virtually all were supporters of the system both in fact and in theory. Few white Southerners spoke against the evils of slavery in the three decades before the Civil War. Their diaries, letters, and sermons showed few pangs of private regret or guilt, seldom mentioning slaves or slavery at all.

White Southerners explained the apparent inconsistency between their freedom and the slavery they oversaw with the words of race. In their eyes, the descendants of the English were naturally fitted for freedom by blood, by heritage, and by struggle. White Southerners explained the bondage of African Americans by bondage itself; because black people were held in slavery they were fit only for slavery. Whites turned to the Bible and to antiquity for sanction of slavery. Whites took the color of skin as evidence of something deeper, of character and depth of feeling and longing for freedom.

The role of slavery in the North's cause was not always clear. As the quotes in this book show, at the beginning of the Civil War few white Northerners proclaimed themselves fighting a war to abolish slavery. They wanted to stop the spread of slavery, to be sure, for they viewed slaveholders as petty tyrants and non-slaveholding white Southerners as dupes for tolerating slavery in their midst. But this distaste and disdain for white Southerners did not translate into respect or even into concern for black Southerners. While those who wanted to begin the end of slavery immediately spoke out in the North from the 1830s on, they were by no means a majority in 1860. Most white Northerners seemed contemptuous of black people, sometimes violently so.

This ambiguity of purpose tore at the Union throughout the war. Abraham Lincoln viewed slavery with deep and genuine distaste, but he wanted above all to win the war and to keep the Union together. Over the course of the war he and some of his generals began to understand that the best way to defeat the Confederacy was to turn slavery, a potential strength of the South, against the enemy. Slavery could be used to help woo English or French support by identifying the North with the cause of freedom. Slavery could be used to weaken the Southern economy by allowing Union generals to accept runaway slaves into their camps. Slavery could be used to strengthen the North by recruiting 180,000 African American soldiers to fight against the Confederates, saving white Northern lives while demonstrating the enormous hunger of black Americans for freedom. Nevertheless, many white Northerners remained skeptical of ending slavery immediately. As late as 1864, only a victory by William T. Sherman in Atlanta ensured that Lincoln would win reelection as president. The man who ran against him, George McClellan, wanted to bring the war to an end, leaving slavery in place.

In sharp contrast, the language of black freedom echoed from the very outset of the conflict among black people themselves. The quotes in this book present their key words: *freedom, liberation, emancipation, rights*. Black people were not sure at the beginning of the war that the conflict would help bring those freedoms, for few white people in the North spoke in those terms. As the war progressed, however, African American leaders used every opportunity to impress upon Union leaders that the cause of Union could best be served by making it the cause of a more universal freedom. Arming black men to fight not only helped on the battlefield, it also helped in the black freedom struggle. Some white Northerners began to talk more of the evils of slavery and to celebrate the general idea of freedom. What that talk might mean remained unclear from one year to the next, however, as events spun out of anyone's control in 1865 and 1866.

Throughout the war, women held the same political ideals as men. Some women seemed even more virulent and vitriolic than their husbands and sons; Northerners certainly accused white Southern women of being so. In other cases, women left to tend farms, plantations, and homes tired of the war earlier than did the men swept up in the camaraderie and excitement of the camp and battlefield. Women were more likely to speak of *mourning, hunger,* and *sacrifice* than their men, to speak more of family and children. For many women true manliness elevated family over political cause. It was no accident that desertion increased in the second half of the war.

The end of war brought no common language to North and South, black and white, male and female. Indeed, the end of the actual fighting seemed to unleash even harsher language. Freed from the common experience of battlefield suffering, Northerners and Southerners seemed to feel mainly contempt and anger toward one another. The Union blamed the South for starting a war that killed more than 600,000 Americans, but the South refused to accept the blame, then or for decades thereafter. In their eyes, Reconstruction showed the true purpose of the North from the very beginning: to destroy the economic and political power of the white South. Those former Confederates could see no purpose in Northern Republican support for black suffrage other than vindictiveness and petty cruelty. White Northerners, for their part, saw their worst opinions of white Southerners displayed in Reconstruction. The unwillingness to accept defeat and emancipation graciously, the North charged, showed the true character of the violent, deceitful, and arrogant South.

African Americans steered between the ambivalence of the white North and the bitterness of the white South as carefully as they could, looking for any opportunity to control their own lives. Black Southerners seized on the chance for political power offered by the North, but also sought to maintain peace with the white people among whom they lived and upon whom they depended for employment. The experiment of Reconstruction proved short-lived, white Southerners resisting with every means, the white North and the white South reconciling with one another at the expense of black Southerners. Within three decades of war's end, white veterans of both the Union and the Confederacy spoke of one another with respect born of common bravery and suffering while permitting segregation and disfranchisement to flourish.

The ambiguity of the war's beginning, fighting, and outcome have allowed Americans to argue about the Civil War for all the generations that have followed. People on both sides idealize the purposes of their ancestors and demean those of their opponents. White Southerners have been most visibly invested in the trappings of the Confederacy and in defending honor and heritage, but white Northerners have been invested as well. The war seems evidence to them of the nation's greatness, of its devotion to the ideals of freedom.

Black Americans, while never forgetful of their freedom and how it arrived, have been skeptical of the claims of both Southern and Northern whites. The differences among these three groups of Americans show little sign of disappearing.

This book can help us see the Civil War more clearly. It does so not by imposing an easy moral on the story, not by offering convenient answers to the persistent and troubling questions about the war's causes and outcomes. Rather, it helps us see that the war was, above all, war. It was confusion as well as certainty. It was self-deception and lying as well as nobility of purpose. It was blood of accident and brutality as well as of sacrifice. The war constantly changed within itself, redefined itself. And that process has not yet ended.

EDWARD L. AYERS,
Hugh P. Kelly Professor of History,
University of Virginia

Brief Timeline
of the Civil War

August 10, 1821 Missouri admitted as a slave state during the administration of James Monroe, 5th president of the United States. The Missouri Compromise of 1820 prohibits slavery elsewhere in the territory of the Louisiana Purchase north of 36° 30', the southern boundary of the state.

July 10, 1850 Millard Fillmore inaugurated as 13th president of the United States after the death of President Zachary Taylor in office on July 9, 1850.

August–September 1850 Senator Henry Clay introduces Senate debate leading to the Compromise of 1850 and the Fugitive Slave Act. The compromise admits California as a free state, creates New Mexico and Utah territories and gives them the option of adopting slavery on admission as states, abolishes the slave trade in the District of Columbia, and levies severe penalties for any individuals who interfere with the capture and return of escaped slaves.

June 5, 1851–April 1, 1852 Harriet Beecher Stowe's novel, *Uncle Tom's Cabin*, is serialized in the Washington anti-slavery paper, the *National Era*. Released in book form on March 20, 1852, the novel sells 10,000 copies in one week and over 300,000 copies that year. Over one million copies are sold in England.

March 4, 1853 Franklin Pierce inaugurated as 14th president of the United States.

May 30, 1854 President Pierce signs the Kansas-Nebraska Act into law. Sponsored by Illinois senator Stephen A. Douglas, the act authorizes the creation of the Kansas and Nebraska territories and voids the Missouri Compromise by placing slave or free status under the doctrine of "popular sovereignty."

March 4, 1857 James Buchanan inaugurated as 15th president of the United States.

March 6, 1857 Chief Justice Taney of the Supreme Court announces the Dred Scott decision in *Scott v. Sandford*, which renders the Missouri Compromise unconstitutional by determining that Congress has no power under the Constitution to forbid slavery in the territories; rules that blacks, not being citizens, cannot bring suits in federal courts; and holds that, as slaves are property, travel to free territories does not alter slave status.

August 21–October 15, 1958 Abraham Lincoln and Stephen A. Douglas participate in seven debates on slavery and issues of race as they compete for Douglas's Senate seat. Douglas defeats Lincoln in the November 1858 election.

October 1859 Radical abolitionist John Bown leads a raid on a federal arsenal at Harpers Ferry. His band is captured; he is hanged December 2.

November 6, 1860 Abraham Lincoln is elected 16th president of the United States.

December 20, 1860 South Carolina votes to secede from the Union. Mississippi, Florida, Alabama, Georgia, Louisiana, and Texas follow suit (January 9–February 1, 1861).

February 4, 1861 The Confederate States of America is established at a Montgomery convention.

April 12, 1861 South Carolina troops bomb Fort Sumter; Union Major Robert Anderson surrenders the fort on April 13.

April 15, 1861 Lincoln calls for 75,000 three-month volunteers.

April 17, 1861 Virginia secedes from the Union. One month later, its capital becomes the capital of the Confederacy.

April 19, 1861 Union orders naval blockade of Confederate coastline.

May 13, 1861 Queen Victoria announces Great Britain's neutrality.

July 21, 1861 First Battle of Bull Run. Confederates under General Pierre Beauregard rout Union troops at Manassas Junction in a battle watched by Washington residents, who had come by carriage, expecting the war to end in one day.

October 21, 1861 Battle of Ball's Bluff. Union roundly defeated.

November 1, 1861 General George McClellan given command of the Union army.

February 25, 1862 Union troops take Nashville without a struggle; Confederacy loses tons of supplies stockpiled there.

March 9, 1862 Battle between the *Monitor* and the *Merrimac* ends in a draw.

March 11, 1862 Because of McClellan's failure to act, Lincoln demotes him to commander of the Army of the Potomac; Union generals now report directly to the secretary of war.

March–May 31, 1862 Union troops advance to outskirts of Richmond, where McClellan awaits reinforcements.

April 1862 Confederate military conscription begins.

April 6–7, 1862 Battle of Shiloh. In Tennessee, advancing Union troops under General Grant turn back Confederate counterattack under General Beauregard.

May 1, 1862 New Orleans falls to Union forces led by Admiral Farragut and General Butler.

June 1, 1862 Robert E. Lee named commander in chief of the Army of Northern Virginia.

June 6, 1862 Memphis falls to Union troops.

June 26–July 2, 1862 Seven Days' battles. Confederates under Lee force Union troops under McClellan to retreat, ending the Union threat to Richmond. Casualties high on both sides.

August 28–30, 1862 Second Battle of Bull Run (Second Manassas). Confederates defeat Union forces under General Pope, a few miles south of Washington.

September 17, 1862 Battle of Antietam. Union forces under McClellan meet Lee's army in Maryland, forcing them to abandon a general invasion of the North. Highest single day of casualties in the war: a combined 23,110 dead, wounded, or missing.

October 8, 1862 Battle of Perryville. Confederate troops under Braxton Bragg fail to gain local support in Kentucky and are forced by Union troops under General Buell to retreat south.

November 5, 1862 Lincoln replaces McClellan with General Burnside.

December 13, 1862 Battle of Fredericksburg. Under Burnside, Union army routed with heavy casualties.

December 31, 1862 Battle of Murfreesboro (Tennessee) begins; inconclusive, heavy casualties.

January 1, 1863 President Lincoln issues the Emancipation Proclamation.

March 3, 1863 Lincoln signs first Conscription Act. Hired substitutes or payments of $300 can be used for exemptions.

May 1863 Bureau of Colored Troops established by the War Department to recruit black soldiers.

May 2–4, 1863 Battle of Chancellorsville. Lee's forces defeat Hooker's Army of the Potomac in a major victory for the Confederacy. Stonewall Jackson mortally wounded by his own troops.

May 22–July 4, 1863 Siege of Vicksburg. Union troops under General Grant attack Vicksburg to take control of the Mississippi. Confederates eventually starved into surrender.

July 1–4, 1863 Battle of Gettysburg. Confederates under General Lee invade Pennsylvania, engaging larger Union force under General Meade. Successive Confederate charges fail to dislodge Union troops, forcing Confederate withdrawal.

July 13–16, 1863 Draft riots. Mobs react violently to the Conscription Act in several cities throughout the Northeast. The worst riots are in New York City, where mostly Irish workingmen attack and lynch blacks.

July 18, 1863 Fort Wagner. The first black regiment, the 54th Massachusetts Volunteers, assault Fort Wagner in Charleston harbor.

November 19, 1863 President Lincoln delivers the Gettysburg Address.

September 19–20, 1863 Battle of Chickamauga Creek. In bloodiest single battle of war, Confederates eventually force Union retreat.

November 23–25, 1863 Battle of Chattanooga. Union troops gain control of Tennessee, opening way into Georgia.

March 9, 1864 General Grant becomes commander of all Union armies.

April 12, 1864 Fort Pillow massacre. General Forrest captures Tennessee fort on the Mississippi; in the aftermath over 300 black and 53 white soldiers are murdered.

May 3, 1864 Grant begins advance into Virginia, driving toward Richmond.

May 4, 1864 Sherman begins the march toward Atlanta.

May 5–6, 1864 Battle of the Wilderness. Bloody but inconclusive battle.

May 8–12, 1864 Battle of Spotsylvania. Attempting to maneuver around Lee, Grant's army is met in this Virginia town; five days of fighting lead to a stalemate.

June 1–3, 1864 Battle of Cold Harbor. Grant assaults Lee's defenses, with heavy losses on both sides.

June 15–18, 1864 Battle of Petersburg. Lee fights off Grant's attack, but Grant settles in to besiege the city.

August 5, 1864 Battle of Mobile Bay. Union ships under Admiral Farragut engage the Confederate fleet and cut off Mobile's link to the sea.

September 2, 1864 Battle of Atlanta. Union troops under General Sherman capture and burn the city.

November 8, 1864 Lincoln wins reelection as president of the United States.

November 14–December 22, 1864 Sherman's March to the Sea. Union troops march from Atlanta to Savannah on Georgia's Atlantic coast, devastating the countryside along the way.

January 31, 1865 Congress passes the Thirteenth Amendment, abolishing slavery. First state (Illinois) ratifies on February 1. The amendment is ratified December 13, 1865.

February 17, 1865 Union troops under General Sherman take and burn Columbia, South Carolina.

February 18, 1865 Union fleet captures Charleston.

March 13, 1865 War-weary Confederacy, weakened by desertions, approves arming of slaves.

April 1, 1865 Battle of Five Forks. In one of the last battles of the war, General Sheridan routs a Confederate force attacking the Union siege of Petersburg.

April 3, 1865 Union forces enter Petersburg and Richmond. U.S. president Lincoln arrives to visit Richmond on April 5, is cheered by the city's former slaves, and sits in Confederate president Davis's chair.

April 9, 1865 Confederate general Robert E. Lee formally surrenders to Union general Ulysses S. Grant at Appomattox Court House in Virginia.

April 14, 1865 John Wilkes Booth assassinates Abraham Lincoln at Ford's Theater. Vice-President Andrew Johnson takes the oath of office April 15 to become the 17th president of the United States.

April 18, 1865 Confederate general Joseph Johnston surrenders to Union general Sherman, marking the formal end of Confederate resistance.

April 16, 1865 John Wilkes Booth is shot and killed.

May 10, 1865 Confederate president Jefferson Davis is captured in Georgia.

May 24–25, 1865 Over 150,000 men participate in the Grand Review through Washington, D.C.

May 29, 1865 President Andrew Johnson issues an Amnesty Proclamation granting pardons to "all persons who have, directly or indirectly, participated in the existing rebellion," excluding certain Confederate leaders.

April 9, 1866 The nation's first Civil Rights Act is passed by the Thirty-ninth Congress over Johnson's veto and provides that "citizens of every race and color, without regard to any previous condition of slavery or involuntary servitude" shall have the same rights "as is enjoyed by white citizens." The act, however, does not extend to Native Americans.

June 13, 1866 The Fourteenth Amendment to the Constitution is passed by Congress. The amendment grants citizenship to "all persons born or naturalized in the United States" and asserts that states may not deprive individuals of "life, liberty, or property without due process of law." The amendment is ratified on July 28, 1868.

March 2, 1867 The First Reconstruction Acts are vetoed by President Johnson and passed by Congress over the veto on the same day.

August 12, 1867 In direct defiance of the Tenure of Office Act, President Andrew Johnson removes Secretary of War Edwin Stanton from office and replaces him with Ulysses S. Grant. Johnson's intent is to control Radical Republicans in Congress and ensure Lincoln's reconstruction and reconciliation policies.

January 3, 1868 Congress orders Stanton reinstated as head of the War Department. When Johnson defiantly replaces Stanton again on February 21, impeachment proceedings are instituted.

March 13, 1868 Chief Justice Salmon P. Chase of the Supreme Court presides over impeachment proceedings brought against President Andrew Johnson. Johnson is acquitted on May 26, 1868, by a margin of one vote.

February 26, 1869 The Fifteenth Amendment to the Constitution is passed by Congress. The amendment guarantees the right to vote shall not be denied "on account of race, color, or previous condition of servitude." It is ratified on March 30, 1870.

March 4, 1869 Ulysses S. Grant, former Union general, is inaugurated as 18th president of the United States.

Part I.
Coming of the War

★ ★ ★

Abraham Lincoln, elected sixteenth president of the United States

Ex-slave, abolitionist, and statesman Frederick Douglass, celebrated in a Reconstruction-era poster

Politics

✦ ✦ ✦

The Fugitive Slave Acts,
The Missouri Compromise, and
The Kansas-Nebraska Act

Slavery has within itself the seeds of its own destruction. Keep it within its limits, let it remain where it now is, and in time it will wear itself out.

David Wilmot, U.S. representative from Pennsylvania,
on his Proviso to keep slavery out of territory
gained from Mexico, 1846

It was the purpose of this Act
To make the Northern States, in fact,
The brutal master's hunting grounds,
To be explored by human hounds
Who would, for shining gold, again
Bind on the bleeding captive's chain.

Elymas Payson Rogers (1815-1861)
"In 'Fifty Congress Passed a Bill,"
on the Fugitive Slave Acts

No more slave States: no slave Territories.

Salmon P. Chase, senator from Ohio,
Platform of the Free Soil National Convention, 1848

You may pass it here. You may send it to the other House. It may become law. But its effect will be to satisfy all thinking men that no compromise with slavery will endure, except so long as they serve the interests of slavery.

Salmon P. Chase, senator from Ohio,
on the Kansas-Nebraska Act, January 30, 1854

I look upon that enactment not as a law, but as a violence from the beginning. It was conceived in violence, passed in violence, is maintained in violence, and is being executed in violence.

Abraham Lincoln, letter to Joshua F. Speed,
on the Kansas-Nebraska Act, August 24, 1855

You promised us bread, and you have given us a stone; you promised us a fish, and you have given us a serpent.

James Mason, senator from Virginia,
angered at Senator Douglas's election-year wavering
on extending slavery into the territories, 1858

Thirty years ago they rubbed out part of the line, and said to [the Slave Trader], "You may go into the lands of the South, but not into the lands of the North." This was the Missouri Compromise. Five years ago they rubbed out the rest of the line, and said to him, "We leave it to the Settlers to decide whether you shall come in or not." This was the Nebraska Bill. Now they turn humbly to him, hat in hand, and say, "Go where you please; the land is all yours, the National flag shall protect you, and the National Troops shoot down whoever resists you." This is the Dred Scott decision.

Pennsylvania newspaper, 1859

I care nothing about that anti-slavery which wants to make the Territories free, while it is unwilling to extend to me, as a man, in the free States, all the rights of a man.

H. Ford Douglass, African American leader from Illinois,
speech to the abolitionists in Framingham,
Massachusetts, July 4, 1860

The very best that can be said of [the Republican] party is, that it is opposed to forcing slavery into any Territory of the United States where the white people of that Territory do not want it . . . That party . . . is simply opposed to allowing slavery to go where it is not at all likely to go.

Frederick Douglass, Douglass' Monthly, September 1860

You slaveholders have lived so long on your plantations with no one to gain-say you and the negroes only look up and worship you that you expect to govern everybody & have it all your own way.

Frances Edmonston to her father and brothers,
noted in her sister Charlotte's diary, November 16, 1860

Great men in the Senate sate,
Sage and hero, side by side,
Building for their sons the State,
Which they shall rule with pride.

They forbore to break the chain
Which bound the dusky tribe,
Checked by the owners' fierce disdain,
Lured by "Union" as the bribe.

Ralph Waldo Emerson (1803–1882), "Voluntaries"

I'd rather every one of my children should be laid out on the cooling board, than to have the Yankees get my niggers.

Georgia mother of four, as recounted by "Miss Abby,"
an Atlanta schoolteacher, May 30, 1864

Abraham Lincoln, Speech on the Kansas-Nebraska Act, 1854

This declared indifference, but as I must think, covert real zeal for the spread of slavery, I cannot but hate. I hate it because of the monstrous injustice of slavery itself. I hate it because it deprives our republican example of its just influence in the world—enables the enemies of free institutions, with plausibility, to taunt us as hypocrites.

Abraham Lincoln, 1854

A white man takes his slave to Nebraska now; who will inform the negro that he is free? Who will take him before court to test the question of his freedom? In ignorance of his legal emancipation, he is kept chopping, splitting, and plowing.

Abraham Lincoln, 1854

I am aware you say that taking slaves from the States to Nebraska, does not make slaves of freemen; but the African slavetrader can say just as much. He does not catch free negroes and bring them here. He finds them already slaves in the hands of their black captors, and he honestly buys them at the rate of about a red cotton handkerchief a head.

Abraham Lincoln, 1854

Repeal the Missouri Compromise—repeal all compromises—repeal the Declaration of Independence—repeal all past history, you still cannot repeal human nature. It still will be the abundance of man's heart, that slavery extension is wrong; and out of the abundance of his heart, his mouth will continue to speak.

Abraham Lincoln, 1854

Our republican robe is soiled, and trailed in the dust. Let us repurify it. Let us turn and wash it white, in the spirit, if not the blood, of the Revolution. Let us turn slavery from its claims of "moral right," back upon its existing legal rights, and its arguments of "necessity." Let us return it to the position our fathers gave it; and there let it rest in peace. Let us re-adopt the Declaration of Independence, and with it, the practices, and policy, which harmonize with it. Let north and south—let all Americans—let all lovers of liberty everywhere—join in the great and good work. If we do this, we shall not only have saved the Union; but we shall have so saved it, as to make, and to keep it, forever worthy of the saving.

Abraham Lincoln, 1854

Stand with anybody that stands right. Stand with him while he is right and part with him when he goes wrong. Stand with the abolitionist in restoring the Missouri Compromise; and stand against him when he attempts to repeal the fugitive slave law. In the latter case you stand with the southern disunionist. What of that? you are still right.

Abraham Lincoln, 1854

Lincoln-Douglas Debates

Does the Judge say it can stand? . . . I would like to know if it is his opinion that a house divided against itself can stand. If he does, then there is a question of veracity, not between him and me, but between the Judge and an authority of a somewhat higher character.

Abraham Lincoln,
first Lincoln-Douglas debate, August 21, 1858

They knew when they framed the Constitution that in a country as wide and broad as this, with such a variety of climate, production, and interest, the people necessarily required different laws and institutions in different localities. They knew that the laws and regulations which would suit the granite hills of New Hampshire would be unsuited to the rice plantations of South Carolina, and they, therefore, provided that each State should retain its own Legislature, and its own sovereignty with the full and complete power to do as it pleased within its own limits, in all that was local and not national.

Stephen Douglas,
first Lincoln-Douglas debate, August 21, 1858

I hold that New York had as much right to abolish slavery as Virginia has to continue it, and that each and every State of this Union is a sovereign power, with the right to do as it pleases upon this question of slavery, and upon all its domestic institutions . . . Now, my friends, if we will only act conscientiously and rigidly upon this great principle of popular sovereignty . . . we will continue to be at peace with one another. Why should Illinois be at war with Missouri, or Kentucky with Ohio, or Virginia with New York, merely because their institutions differ?

Stephen Douglas,
first Lincoln-Douglas debate, August 21, 1858

Why can it not exist divided into free and slave States? Washington, Jefferson, Franklin, Madison, Hamilton, Jay, and the great men of that day, made this Government divided into free States and slave States, and left each State perfectly free to do as it pleased on the subject of slavery. Why can it not exist on the same principles on which our fathers made it?

Stephen Douglas,
first Lincoln-Douglas debate, August 21, 1858

Any one of you gentlemen might as well say to a son twelve years old that he is big enough, and must not grow any larger, and in order to prevent his growth, put a hoop around him to keep him to his present size. What would be the result? Either the hoop must burst and be rent asunder, or the child must die. So it would be with this great nation. With our natural increase, growing with a rapidity unknown in any other part of the globe, with the tide of emigration that is fleeing from despotism in the Old World to seek refuge in our own, there is a constant torrent pouring into this country that requires more land, more territory upon which to settle; and just as fast as our interest and our destiny require additional territory in the North, in the South, or on the islands of the ocean, I am for it, and when we acquire it, will leave the people, according to the Nebraska Bill, free to do as they please on the subject of slavery and every other question.

Stephen Douglas, in debate with Abraham Lincoln
for the Senate seat, 1858

Political Debate

A little rebellion now and then is a good thing.

Thomas Jefferson, letter to James Madison, January 30, 1787

Our Federal Union: it must be preserved.

Andrew Jackson, toast given
on the Jefferson Birthday Celebration, April 13, 1830

The advice nearest to my heart and deepest in my convictions is, that the Union of the states be cherished and perpetuated. Let the open enemy of it be regarded as a Pandora with her box opened, and the disguised one as the serpent creeping with his deadly wiles into Paradise.

James Madison, *Advice to My Country*

Without union our independence and liberty would never have been achieved; without union they never can be maintained. Divided into twenty-four, or even a smaller number, of separate communities, we shall see our internal trade burdened with numberless restraints and exactions; communication between distant points and sections obstructed or cut off; our sons made soldiers to deluge with blood the fields they now till in peace; the mass of our people borne down and impoverished by taxes to support armies and navies, and military leaders at the head of their victorious legions becoming our law-givers and judges.

Andrew Jackson, second Inaugural Address,
March 4, 1833

The Union forever, Hurrah! boys, Hurrah!
Down with the traitor, up with the stars;
While we rally round the flag, boys, rally once again,
Shouting the battle cry of Freedom.

George Frederick Root (1820-1895),
"The Battle-Cry of Freedom"

At what point then is the approach of danger to be expected? I answer, if it ever reach us, it must spring up amongst us. It cannot come from abroad. If destruction be our lot, we must ourselves be its author and finisher. As a nation of freemen, we must live through all time, or die by suicide.

Abraham Lincoln, 1838

The compact which exists between the North and the South is a covenant with death and an agreement with hell.

William Lloyd Garrison,
resolution of the Anti-Slavery Society, 1843

White or black, if a citizen of Maine, we must treat him as a citizen. The folly of such a claim is only equaled by the recklessness with which the pre-tension is urged . . . A negro, born in Maine, is no better than one born here, and if he comes here, he must abide by our negro laws. Were not this so, this State might be infested with runaway negroes, who, having acquired the rights of citizens in Maine, would return to beard their masters and claim the protection of the federal Constitution.

Report of a committee of the South Carolina legislature
on laws respecting African American seamen, 1844

I have heard something said about allegiance to the South. I know no South, no North, no East, no West, to which I owe any allegiance.

Henry Clay, speech on the Senate floor, 1848

The cry of Union! Union! the glorious Union! can no more prevent disunion, than the cry of Health! health! glorious Health! on the part of the physician can save a patient lying dangerously ill. So long as the Union, instead of being regarded as a protector, is regarded in the opposite character by not much less than a majority of the states, it will be in vain to attempt to conciliate them by pronouncing eulogies on it.

John C. Calhoun, senator from South Carolina, March 1850

This government, with its institutions, belongs to the people who inhabit it. Whenever they shall grow weary of the existing government, they can exercise their constitutional right of amending it, or their revolutionary right to dismember or overthrow it.

Abraham Lincoln, First Republican State Convention,
Illinois, 1856 (quoted by Theodore Roosevelt at
the Ohio Constitutional Convention, 1912)

All this talk about the dissolution of the Union is humbug—nothing but folly.

Abraham Lincoln, 1856

We have had the Union saved five or six different times within my day, and it is the only thing I ever knew to suffer by salvation.

Ben Wade, congressman from Ohio, on compromises
forced by the South with the threat of secession, 1856

A house divided against itself cannot stand. I believe this government cannot endure, permanently half slave and half free. I do not expect the Union to be dissolved—I do not expect the house to fall—but I do expect it will cease to be divided. It will become all one thing or all the other.

Abraham Lincoln,
speech at the Republican State Convention, June 16, 1858

I admit that I am ambitious, and would like to be president . . . but there is no such good luck in store for me.

Abraham Lincoln, on losing Senate election, 1858

Surely no native-born woman loves her country better than I love America. The blood of one of its Revolutionary patriots flows in my veins, and it is the Union for which he pledged "life, fortune, and sacred honor" that I love, not any divided, or special section of it.

G., a pro-Union woman from New Orleans,
diary entry, December 1, 1860

If the Union can only be maintained by new concessions to the slaveholders; if it can only be stuck together and held together by a new drain on the negro's blood; if the North is to forswear the exercise of all rights incompatible with the safety and perpetuity of slavery, . . . then will every right minded man and woman in the land say, let the Union perish, and perish forever.

Frederick Douglass, *Douglass' Monthly*, January 1861

I am for the Union without any "if."

Sam Houston, governor of Texas,
deposed after secession, February 1861

When any one State in the American Union refuses obedience to the Confederation by which they have bound themselves, the rest have a natural right to compel obedience.

Thomas Jefferson, *Writings*, Vol. XVII

This Union is worth more than all the niggers that ever trod the shore of Africa or made cotton below Mason and Dixon's line.

> Reporter from the *Sacramento Union*,
> urging compromise with the South, February 13, 1861

If, by the mere force of numbers, a majority should deprive a minority of any clearly written constitutional right, it might, in a moral point of view, justify revolution—certainly would, if such right were a vital one. But such is not our case.

> Abraham Lincoln, first Inaugural Address, March 4, 1861

A majority, held in restraint by constitutional checks, and limitations, and always changing easily, with deliberate changes of popular opinions and sentiments, is the only true sovereign of a free people. Whoever rejects it, does, of necessity, fly to anarchy or to despotism.

> Abraham Lincoln, first Inaugural Address, March 4, 1861

The Constitution, in all its provisions, looks to an indestructible Union composed of indestructible States.

> Salmon P. Chase, decision in *Texas* v. *White*, 7 Wallace 725

Physically speaking, we cannot separate. We cannot remove our respective sections from each other, nor build an impassable wall between them. A husband and wife may be divorced, and go out of the presence, and beyond the reach of each other; but the different parts of our country cannot do this.

> Abraham Lincoln, first Inaugural Address, March 4, 1861

Today I was pressed into service to make red flannel cartridge-bags for ten-inch columbiads. I basted while Mrs. S. sewed, and I felt ashamed to think that I had not the moral courage to say, "I don't approve of your war and won't help you, particularly in the murderous part of it."

G., a pro-Union woman from New Orleans,
diary entry, May 10, 1861

We can't go a broken Union or tearing out the stripes, or putting out the stars in the flag. We are too proud and vain of the "greatest nation in all creation" to see it broken up and reduced to a series of petty and ever jarring republics or military despotisms.

Sacramento Union, May 28, 1861

A thoughtful mind, when it sees a nation's flag, sees not the flag only, but the nation itself; and whatever may be its symbols, its insignias, he reads chiefly in the flag the government, the principles, the truths, the history which belongs to the nation that sets it forth.

Henry Ward Beecher, "The National Flag," 1861

It forces us to ask: "Is there, in all republics, this inherent, fatal weakness?" "Must a government, of necessity, be too strong for the liberties of its own people, or too weak to maintain its own existence?"

Abraham Lincoln, on secession,
message to Congress in special session, July 4, 1861

The men and women of the North are slaveholders, those of the South slaveowners. The guilt rests on the North equally with the South.

Susan B. Anthony, "No Union with Slaveholders"

Masters have tried to make us believe that the Yankees only wished to sell us to Cuba, to get money to carry on the war.

Slave, regarding Confederate propaganda, September 1861

I am a Virginian, every drop of blood that flows in my veins is Virginian, but my being Virginian, don't make me a Secessionist—it, on the contrary, makes me a Unionist, for I think Va's good, is in holding to the Union, to the Constitution & to the Laws.

Sallie Pendleton Van Rensselaer,
from what would become West Virginia, January 6, 1862

I am not of Virginia's blood; she is of mine.

Joshua Chamberlain, Union general

Thou, too, sail on, O Ship of State!
Sail on, O Union, strong and great!
Humanity with all its fears,
With all the hopes of future years,
Is hanging breathless on thy fate!

Henry Wadsworth Longfellow (1807–1882),
"The Building of the Ship"

I am simply fighting for the Union as it was given to us. I want nothing more. I will have nothing less.

George Avery, Union soldier,
letter to his future wife, January 26, 1862

Opposition is not tolerated north of the Potomac, and any man who attempts it will be dealt with as a traitor . . . The old Constitution of the United States has sunk into absolute contempt. Those who express a wish to see it respected, are forthwith clapped into jail on a charge of treason.

Southern Illustrated News, October 11, 1862

This war be worse I reckon . . . for everybody is killing everybody.

Aunt Sally, 95-year-old ex-slave,
when asked which war was worse—the Civil War
or the Revolutionary War, 1863

You do not want to see this union and all our liberties taken from us and I
stand by and not lift my hand to save it.

Caleb Blanchard, Union soldier,
letter to his wife, January 18, 1863

You know I have never agreed with you in politics, but permit me to say one
thing: Prosecute this war with the utmost vigor and put down this accursed rebellion against God and man and posterity north and south will bless you forever.

William H. Underwood,
letter to Abraham Lincoln, December 6, 1863

The illusion that times that were are better than those that are, has probably
pervaded all ages.

Horace Greeley, "The American Conflict," 1864

Let's have the Union restored as it was, if we can; but if we can't, I'm in favor
of the Union as it wasn't.

Artemus Ward (1834-1867), journalist

Heterogeneous populations, hostile systems, and irreconcilable ideas had
only been . . . held to a bare juxta-position by a constitutional compact. No
chemical union had ever taken place; for that the white-hot crucible of civil
war was found necessary.

William Grosvenor, journalist, after the war

Outside of our financial and mercantile arrangements the Union is all incomplete. Our fathers never finished their work. The Founders left the United States to float like a balloon in the air . . . the time is now to complete the machine which our father left incomplete.

Wendell Phillips, abolitionist, after the war

Echoes

The coming of the American Civil War is a case study in democracy's limitations.

William Freehling, historian

The "Union"—which we rarely refer to as a union any more, so obvious is the fact—gives us our most significant sense of identity, limited as that may be, and the best and most inclusive hope for our future, and that of mankind.

Robert Penn Warren, *The Legacy of the Civil War*

In This Temple
As In The Hearts Of The People
For Whom He Saved The Union
The Memory Of Abraham Lincoln
Is Enshrined Forever

Inscription, the Lincoln Memorial, Washington, D.C.

Abolitionist, leader of the raid on Harpers Ferry

John Brown

Caution, sir! I am eternally tired of hearing that word caution. It is nothing but the word of cowardice!

John Brown, response to a neighbor's warning

I don't think the people of the slave states will ever consider the subject of slavery in its true light till some other argument is resorted to than moral persuasion.

John Brown, October 1859

Men who live by robbing their fellow-men of their labor and liberty . . . have by the single act of slaveholding voluntarily placed themselves beyond the laws of justice and honor . . . it can never be wrong for the imbruted and whip-scarred slaves, or their friends, to hunt, to harass, and even strike down the traffickers in human flesh.

Frederick Douglass, 1859

When I strike, the bees will begin to swarm, and I want you to help hive them.

John Brown to Frederick Douglass,
before the raid on Harpers Ferry, October 1859

Had I so interfered in behalf of the rich, the powerful, the intelligent, the so-called great, or in behalf of any of their friends . . . and suffered and sacrificed what I have in this interference . . . every man in this court would have deemed it worthy of reward rather than punishment.

John Brown, at his sentencing, November 2, 1859

Believing in peace principles, I cannot sympathize with the method you chose to advance the cause of freedom. But I honor your generous intentions—I admire your courage, moral and physical . . . I reverence you for the humanity which tempered your zeal. I sympathize with you in your cruel bereavement, your sufferings, and your wrongs. In brief, I love you and I bless you.

Lydia Maria Child, letter to John Brown

He was a superior man. He did not value bodily life in comparison with ideal things. He did not recognize unjust human laws; but resisted them as he was bid. For once we are lifted out of the trivialness and dust of politics into the region of truth and manhood.

Henry David Thoreau, "A Plea for Captain John Brown," 1859

If it is deemed necessary that I should forfeit my life for the furtherance of the ends of justice, and mingle my blood further with the blood of my children

and with the blood of millions in this slave country whose rights are disre-
garded by wicked, cruel, and unjust enactments—I submit; so let it be done.

John Brown, at his sentencing, November 2, 1859

In the name of the young girl sold from the warm clasp of a mother's arms to
the clutches of a libertine or a profligate, in the name of the slave mother, her
heart rocked to and fro by the agony of her mournful separations, I thank you,
that you have been brave enough to reach out your hands to the crushed and
blighted of my race.

Black woman from Indiana, letter to John Brown, December 1859

This *is* a beautiful country.

John Brown, riding to the gallows
seated on his coffin, December 2, 1859

So perish all such enemies of Virginia! All such enemies of the Union! All
such foes of the human race!

Colonel Preston of the Virginia militia,
to the assembled crowd at the hanging, December 2, 1859

Hanging from the beam,
Slowly swaying (such the law),
Gaunt the shadow on your green,
        Shenandoah!
The cut is on the crown
(Lo, John Brown),
And the stabs shall heal no more.

Herman Melville (1819–1891), "The Portent"

John Brown died on a scaffold for the slave;
Dark was the hour when we dug his hallowed grave;
Now God avenges the life he gladly gave,
Freedom reigns today!

"The President's Proclamation,"
sung to the tune of "Battle Hymn of the Republic"

Let Virginia make him a martyr. His soul was noble; his work miserable. But a cord and a gibbet would redeem all that, and round up Brown's failure with a heroic success.

Henry Ward Beecher, abolitionist preacher,
exhorting his congregation not to pray for
John Brown's deliverance, 1859

Old John Brown . . . agreed with us in thinking slavery wrong. That cannot excuse violence, bloodshed, and treason. It could avail him nothing that he might think himself right.

Abraham Lincoln

Nobody was ever more justly hanged.

Nathaniel Hawthorne

I hear many condemn these men because they were so few. When were the good and the brave ever in a majority?

Henry David Thoreau, "A Plea for Captain John Brown," 1859

It was not a slave insurrection. It was an attempt by white men to get up a revolt among slaves, in which the slaves refused to participate. In fact, it was so absurd, that the slaves, with all their ignorance, saw plainly that it could not succeed.

Abraham Lincoln,
address to the Cooper Institute, February 27, 1860

And Old Brown,
Old Osawatomie Brown,
May trouble you more than ever, when you've nailed his coffin down!

Anderson's *A Voice From Harpers Ferry*

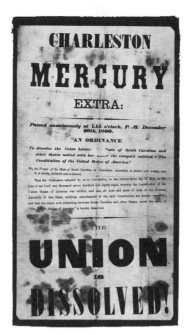

Headline, Charleston Mercury

Secession and the Confederacy

Secession

The South was slowly strengthening itself to do one of two things, to control the government in favor of the spread & sway of slavery, or to acquire such coherency & vigor as to break away & assert its separate independence.

William H. Seward, U.S. secretary of state,
on the South in the 1840s

Let us employ our own teachers, especially that they may teach our own doctrines. Let us dress in the wool raised on our own pastures. Let us eat the flour from our own mills, and if we can't get that, why let us go back to our old accustomed corn bread.

> Henry A. Wise, governor of Virginia,
> welcoming home Southern medical students who left
> Northern schools in the aftermath of John Brown's raid, December 22, 1859

Doubly justified by the absence of wrong on our part, and by wanton aggression on the part of others, there can be no doubt that the courage and patriotism of the people of the Confederate States will be found equal to any measures of defense which honor and security may require.

> Jefferson Davis, Inaugural Address, February 18, 1860

The union now subsisting between South Carolina and other States, under the name of "The United States of America," is hereby dissolved.

> Ordinance of Secession, issued by delegates
> of the South Carolina Convention, December 20, 1860

Oh, it is all folly, madness, a crime against civilization.

> William T. Sherman, Union general, on receiving word of the
> secession of South Carolina, December 24, 1860

You can never subjugate us; you never can convert the free sons of the soil into vassals, paying tribute to your power, and you never, never can degrade them to the level of an inferior and servile race. Never! Never!

> Judah Benjamin, senator from Louisiana,
> bidding farewell to the Senate, December 31, 1860

In December 1860, the question was whether there was a sufficient cause for dissolving the Union. In February following, the question was, shall Tennessee secede? In May, it was, what shall I, as an individual, do? Shall I go with my state into secession, or shall I remain true to the old government?

> Oliver P. Temple, former slaveholder from Tennessee,
> explaining the momentum of events in the South, 1899

I rise, Mr. President, for the purpose of announcing to the Senate that I have satisfactory evidence that the State of Mississippi, by a solemn ordinance of her people in convention assembled, has declared her separation from the United States. Under these circumstances, of course, my functions are terminated here. It has seemed to me proper, however, that I should appear in the Senate to announce that fact to my associates, and I will say but very little more.

Jefferson Davis, speech on the floor of the U.S. Senate,
January 21, 1861 (Mississippi is sixth to secede, after South Carolina,
Alabama, Florida, Georgia, and Louisiana, in that order)

The despot's heel is on they shore, Maryland!
His torch is at they temple door, Maryland!
Avenge the patriotic gore
That flecked the streets of Baltimore,
And be the battle-queen of yore, Maryland! my Maryland!

James Ryder Randall (1839-1908), "My Maryland,"
commemorating the firing of Massachusetts troops
on the Baltimore mob that attacked them as they
marched to the front, April 19, 1861, and calling
for Maryland to join the Confederacy

Throughout the entire state men went as emissaries of Secession and told the people they must go out of the Union if they did not wish to be deprived of their slaves and rifles by the "Yankees" who would compel them to perform all menial offices . . . they would exchange position with their negroes and the latter be made their masters.

Junius Browne, war correspondent to the *New York Tribune*,
on secessionist tactics in Arkansas, 1865

Two years, and an abyss of horror and hatred, and the blood of our slaughtered brothers crying aloud from the ground, all prohibit that impious union.

Richmond Enquirer, rejecting the idea of reunion, 1863

Debate

[I would] welcome the intelligence tomorrow. . . that the slaves had risen in the South, and that the sable arms which had been engaged in beautifying and adorning the South, were engaged in spreading death and devastation.

> Frederick Douglass, on whether or not violence
> would be necessary to achieve emancipation

Meanwhile, with perplexed and laggard steps, the United States government followed in the footsteps of the black slave.

> W.E.B. Du Bois, on how the government was forced to deal with
> emancipation in dealing with the threat of secession

We have heard that threat until we are fatigued with the sound. We consider it now, let me say, as mere brutum fulcrum, noise and nothing else.

> William Fessenden, senator from Maine,
> on talk of secession, 1854

We will resist . . . we will sacrifice our lives, burn our houses, and convert our sunny South . . . into a wilderness waste . . . We of the South will tear this Constitution to pieces, and look to our guns for justice.

> Reuben Davis, U.S. representative from Mississippi,
> to Congress, 1860

Peaceable secession is an utter impossibility.

> Daniel Webster, February 1860

If we wait for Alabama, we will wait eternally.

> Lawrence Keitt, South Carolina congressman,
> letter to South Carolina representative W. P. Miles,
> arguing that their state should secede, October 3, 1860

[W]omen who had never before concerned themselves with politics, took the daily papers to their rooms . . . and wept over them.

Mary Ashton Livermore, abolitionist

Mr. Western and Mr. Grafton did not hesitate to say they would be glad to see the country divided—that there was no similarity of interest in the two sections North and South—no love between them and the sooner separated the better . . . Dear Pa charged me to avoid political discussions but goodness alive! how can I sit quietly and hear such talk as this?

Johanna Underwood, Kentucky

Let each State stand firmly by that great constitutional right, let each State mind its own business and let its neighbors alone, and there will be no trouble on this question. If we will stand by that principle, then Mr. Lincoln will find that this republic can exist forever divided into free and slave States, as our fathers made it and the people of each State have decided.

Stephen Douglas

We are without doubt on the verge, on the brink of an abyss into which I do not wish to look.

Alexander Stephens, future vice-president of the Confederacy,
after Lincoln's election, November 6, 1860

If there is sufficient manliness at the South to strike for our rights, honor, and safety, in God's name let it be done before the inauguration of Lincoln.

Milton F. Perry, governor of Florida, November 9, 1860

Stand not upon the order of your going, but go at once . . . There is no union of idea and interests in this country, and there can be no union between freedom and slavery.

H. Ford Douglass, African American leader
from Illinois, November 1860

If the South goes to war for slavery, slavery is doomed in this country. To say so is like opposing one drop to a roaring torrent.

G., a pro-Union woman from New Orleans,
diary entry, December 1, 1860

The prospect before us in regard to our Slave Property, if we continue to remain in the Union, is nothing less than utter ruin.

J. B. Grimball, South Carolina landowner,
diary entry, December 17, 1860

The Southern states ought to split this glorious Union and leave Old Lincoln to preside over the white niggers at the North.

C. L. Burn, South Carolina, 1860

The North can make a steam engine, locomotive or railway car; hardly a yard of cloth or a pair of shoes can you make. You are rushing into war with one of the most powerful, ingeniously mechanical and determined people on earth—right at your doors. You are bound to fail. Only in spirit and determination are you prepared for war. In all else you are totally unprepared, with a bad cause to start with.

William T. Sherman, Union general, on receiving word of the
secession of South Carolina, December 24, 1860

Will you suffer yourself to be spit upon in this way? Are you submissionists to the dictation of South Carolina . . . are you to be called cowards because you do not follow the crazy lead of that crazy state?

Herald, Wilmington, North Carolina,
to anti-secessionist North Carolinians early in 1861

I am one of those dull creatures that cannot see the good of secession.

Robert E. Lee, Confederate general, 1861

This step, secession, once taken, can never be recalled. We and our posterity shall see our lovely South desolated by the demon of war.

Alexander Stephens, future vice-president of the
Confederacy, January 18, 1861

Disunion will be her ruin—for if there is war—it will surely be in the South and the whole land desolated and laid in waste and slavery will certainly go if the Union is dissolved.

Johanna Underwood, Kentucky

It will probably end the war.

Alexander Stephens, vice-president of the Confederacy,
on the secession of Virginia, April 17, 1861

The day we seceded the star of our glory set.

New Orleans gentleman, in reply to boasts about the
grandeur of the new Confederacy, reported in the diary of G.,
a pro-Union woman from New Orleans, April 20, 1861

I think the South is committing suicide, but my lot is cast with the South and
being unable to manage the ship, I intend to face the breakers manfully, and
go down with my companions.

Jonathan Worth, North Carolinian opponent
of secession, May 1861

Mrs. Davis had a small levee to-day in right of her position as wife of the
President. Several ladies there probably looked forward to the time when their
states might secede from the new Confederation, and then afford them the
pleasure of holding a reception. Why not Presidents of the State of Georgia,
or Alabama? Why not King of South Carolina, or Emperor of Florida?

William Howard Russell, correspondent to the *London Times*,
letter from Montgomery, May 1861

Now, in present phraseology, "Confederate" means anything that is rough,
unfinished, unfashionable, or poor. You hear of Confederate dresses, which
means last year's. Confederate bridle means a rope halter, Confederate silver, a
tin cup or spoon. Confederate flour is corn meal, etc.

Sarah Morgan, Baton Rouge

The Southern Confederacy is at present a sad country; but President Davis is
a good and wise man, and many of the generals and other officers in the army
are pious. Then there are many good praying people in the land; so we may
hope that our cause will prosper.

The Geographical Reader for Dixie Children, 1863

So shall the whole rebellious race of Aristocrats bite the dust and bow before
the victorious march of Northern freemen.

Union soldier, writing from Tennessee, January 1863

The prejudice now felt against them for bearing on their persons the brand of slaves, cannot die out immediately.

> Charles L. Reason, African American abolitionist,
> on the trials that would be imposed upon freemen

Go quickly and help fill up the first colored regiment from the North . . . The case is before you. This is our golden opportunity. Let us accept it . . . Let us win for ourselves the gratitude of the country, and the best blessings of our posterity through all time.

> Frederick Douglass, in an 1863 speech,
> encouraged by the Northern response to secession

Child! Have patience! It takes a great while to turn about this great ship of State.

> Sojourner Truth, upon hearing radical abolitionists
> claim that Lincoln moved too slowly on the issues

History fails to tell us of ten millions of freemen being enslaved, who had determined to be free. A braver or more patriotic army than we have, never followed their chief to victory . . . Such men as these, were never born to be slaves.

> John Paris, chaplain, on why the Confederacy
> would yet triumph, February 1864

Our cause is righteous and must prevail.

> McGowan's Brigade, South Carolina volunteers,
> resolution, 1865

Government

Jeff Davis no seceder.

Badge worn by Jefferson Davis's wife, Varina Summer, 1860

I thought Magrath and all those fellows were great apes for resigning and have done it myself. It is an epidemic and very foolish. It reminds me of the Japanese who when insulted rip open their own bowels.

James H. Hammond, South Carolina,
regretting his resignation from the U.S. Senate,
letter to a relative, November 14, 1860

It is no light thing to be told daily by your fellow-citizens, by your fellow-representatives, by your fellow-senators, that you are guilty of the one damning sin that cannot be forgiven. All this they could partly moderate, partly rebuke, and partly bear as long as political power remained in their hands; but they have gradually felt that that was going, and were prepared to cut the rope and run as soon as it was gone.

Anthony Trollope, explaining secession to British readers

I would be an equal, or a corpse.

David Clopton, U.S. representative from Alabama,
letter to Alabama senator Clement Clay, December 13, 1860

We have just carried an election on principles fairly stated to the people. Now we are told in advance, the government shall be broken up, unless we surrender to those we have beaten . . . If we surrender, it is the end of us.

Abraham Lincoln, on a compromise proposal
before Congress, 1861

Weld them together while they are hot.

> William Trescott, South Carolina, on setting up
> a confederacy of seceded states, January 14, 1861

I really feel like I was called on to build a great edifice in a short time without any tools or materials to work with.

> Robert H. Smith, Alabama delegate to the
> Confederate Convention, January 31, 1861

We are without machinery, without means and threatened by a powerful opposition; but I do not despond, and will not shrink from the task imposed on me.

> Jefferson Davis, letter to his wife, February 1861

Although a revolutionary government, none was ever so much under the domination of red tape as the one in Richmond. The martinets who controlled it were a good deal like the hero of Molière's comedy, who complained that his antagonist had wounded him by thrusting him in *carte*, when, according to the rule, it should have been in *tierce*. I cared nothing for the form of a thrust if it brought blood. I did not play with foils.

> Major John Singleton Mosby, on the Confederacy

Big-man-me-ism reigns supreme & every one thinks every other a jealous fool, or an aspiring knave.

> James H. Hammond, former senator of South Carolina,
> of the Confederate Convention, February 6, 1861

We may be kept down by force of arms, but the cement has not been discovered that can make whole the broken vase of the Union.

> James T. Harrison, Mississippi, February 17, 1861

The mountain labors and brings forth a mouse.

> Alexander Stephens, vice-president of the Confederacy,
> complaining of the futility of the Confederate
> Congress, March 1863

My wildest imagination will not picture Mr. Mason as a diplomat. He will say "chaw" for "chew," and he will call himself "Jeems," and he will wear a dress coat to breakfast.

> Mary Chesnut, of James Mason,
> the Confederate commissioner to the Court of St. James

If they had to draw soldiers rations while they staid in Richmond I think they would hurry through a little faster.

> Confederate soldier, on the inaction of the
> Confederate Congress, January 1864

Our Congress are a set of blockheads.

> Isaac Alexander, Confederate soldier, February 21, 1864

Our members of Congress have plenty to do,
But it's seldom, if ever, they do it, 'tis true.

> Confederate war song

[Secession] is an issue which can only be tried by war and decided by victory.

> Abraham Lincoln, message to Congress, 1864

Rebels and Traitors

Rebel is a sacred name;
Traitor, too, is glorious;
By such names our fathers fought—
By them were victorious.

Washington a rebel was,
Jefferson a traitor,
But their treason won success,
And made their glory greater.

Confederate war song

The traitor deserves hemp, and South Carolina is a traitor.

Reverend George Junkin, president of Washington College
(later Washington and Lee) in Lexington, Virginia,
on the secession of South Carolina, 1860

It might seem, at first thought, to be of little difference whether the present movement at the South be called "secession" or "rebellion." The movers, however, well understood the difference. At the beginning, they knew they could never raise their treason to any respectable magnitude, by any name which implies violation of the law.

Abraham Lincoln, message to Congress
in special session, July 4, 1861

We have treated them as misled long enough. Now then let us treat them as the Rebels they are.

Rufus Mead Jr., Union soldier,
letter to his family, May 1862

Away down South in the land of traitors,
Rattlesnakes and alligators,

Right away, come away, right away, come away.
Where cotton's king and men are chattels,
Union boys will win the battles,
Right away, come away, right away, come away.

"Union Dixie"

What a humbug except the brave armies, & the earnest women has this whole affair been. I opposed it *ab initio* but, even with a halter in the distant prospect for I have never thought myself anything but a rebel, I did not think it honorable to leave my own state in such a time.

Benjamin S. Ewell, Confederate staff officer
and former president of William and Mary, speaking at the
end of the war of the Confederacy's try for independence

Living On

Historians have wondered in recent years why the Confederacy did not endure longer. In considerable measure, I would suggest, it was because so many women did not want it to. The way in which their interests in the war were publicly defined—in a very real sense denied—gave women little reason to sustain the commitment modern war required. It may well have been because of its women that the South lost the Civil War.

Drew Gilpin Faust, historian

Such a hue and cry—whose fault? Everybody blamed by somebody else. Only the dead heroes left stiff and stark on the battlefield escape.

Mary Chesnut, on the fall of the Confederacy

The God of Battles has pronounced an irreversible judgment, after a long, desperate, and sanguinary struggle, and it would be neither politic nor patriotic ever again to invoke a new trial of the fearful issue.

J. L. Orr, governor of South Carolina,
address to the legislature, October 1865

The day of the sectionalist is over. The day of the nationalist has come.

Henry Watterson, tribute to "The Nation's Dead,"
Nashville, Tennessee, Memorial Day 1877

I yield to no one precedence in love for the South. But because I love the South, I rejoice in the failure of the Confederacy.

Woodrow Wilson, as a law student at UVA, 1880

Echoes

We had pride and patriotism to spare, but we couldn't feed the living, or raise again our dead!

John Deering, on why the South lost,
in *Lee and His Cause*, 1907

We receive the decision with distaste and apprehension. But it is too late to secede and start another war between the states.

Charleston News & Courier,
on the *Brown* v. *Board of Education* decision, 1954

If the current regime continues its tyranny, we shall not hesitate to advocate secession and self-rule for the Southern states.

Michael Hill, history professor
and president of the Southern League, 1995

Confederate general Robert E. Lee and sons

The War Begins

I see every chance of a long, confused and disorganizing civil war, and I feel no desire to take a hand therein.

William T. Sherman, Union general,
letter to his wife, January 1861

It is our wisest policy to accept it as a declaration of war.

The Charleston *Mercury*,
on Lincoln's first Inaugural Address, March 1861

You rejoiced at the occasion, and only were troubled that there were not three times as many killed in the affair. You were in evident glee—there was no sorrow for the killed nor for the peace of Virginia disturbed—you were rejoicing that by charging Republicans with this thing you might get an advantage of us.

Abraham Lincoln, on the Democrats' opinion
of the raid on Harpers Ferry, March 6, 1860

How we can get along without fighting in the midst of all this lawlessness is impossible for me to see.

Abner Doubleday, Union captain (later general),
letter to his wife from Fort Sumter, April 2, 1861

The firing on that fort will inaugurate a civil war greater than any the world has yet seen . . . you will lose us every friend at the North. You will wantonly strike a hornet's nest which extends from mountains to ocean. Legions now quiet will swarm out and sting us to death. It is unnecessary. It puts us in the wrong. It is fatal.

Robert Toombs, Confederate secretary of state,
to Jefferson Davis, on firing on Fort Sumter, April 1861

She thinks that the taking of Ft. Sumter will put an end to hostilities as the North will see that the South is in earnest, & is so very unwilling to fight, itself!!! She will open her eyes a little when she arrives here & finds ever man of her acquaintance enlisted.

Sarah Butler Wister, a Union sympathizer,
of her sister, a Confederate sympathizer, April 1861

The gage is thrown down and we accept the challenge. We will meet the invader, and God and Battle must decide the issue between the hirelings of Abolition hate and Northern tyranny, and the people of South Carolina defending their freedom and their homes.

Charleston *Mercury*, on the government's intention
to resupply Fort Sumter, April 1861

I could not fire the first gun of the war.

> Roger Pryor, staunch secessionist from Virginia,
> on being offered the honor of firing the first shot
> on Fort Sumter, April 12, 1861

Oh my poor children in the South! Now they will suffer! God knows how they will suffer . . . Oh to think that I should have lived to see the day when Brother should rise against Brother.

> Indiana woman, with children in both the North and South,
> on hearing of the firing on Fort Sumter, April 1861

As yet there was little bloodshed, the old respect for law and confidence in the processes of reason could not at once die, and men still endeavored to convince each other by argument while holding the pistol to each other's heads.

> J. W. DeForest, Union veteran and novelist,
> describing the Spring of 1861

A horse on Sullivan's Island was the only living creature deprived of life during the bombardment.

> Report of the *Charleston Press*,
> on the Battle of Fort Sumter, April 12, 1861

Fort Sumter has surrendered there is nobody hurt.

> W. H. Denslow, telegraph to Abraham Lincoln, April 13, 1861

Quarters in Sumter all burned down. White flag up. Anderson surrenders.

> Dispatches from Fort Sumter, read to a crowd from
> a window of Government House in Montgomery, April 13, 1861

You have won your spurs.

L. P. Walker, Confederate secretary of war,
to General Beauregard, April 13, 1861

April 13. Here begins a new chapter of my journal entitled WAR.

George T. Strong, New York City,
upon hearing the news

The ball has opened. War is inaugurated.

New York Times, April 13, 1861

Never had the Revolutionary fathers received such a workout.

Mark Wahlgren Summers, historian, on the invoking
of the Founding Fathers to rouse patriotic spirit

We propose an appropriation of one million dollars to pay for the scalps of rebels.

Member of the Ohio House of Representatives, April 14, 1861

I am for a war that will either establish or overthrow a Govt., and will purify the atmosphere of political life. We need such a war & we have it now.

John Sherman, U.S. senator from Ohio, April 15, 1861

We shall grow the stronger and the nobler by the very contest we are compelled to wage.

New York Times, April 16, 1861

Nobody seemed to know exactly what it was about, but it was the fashion to be excited.

James M. Morgan, *Recollections of a Rebel Reefer*,
on Montgomery in the week after the firing on Fort Sumter

All good Carolinians are entitled to take the rank of Colonel if they have property enough. In Alabama, if the boat takes a hundred bales from a man's plantation, he is a Colonel. Before the war it required from three hundred to a thousand bales to make him a general.

Miriam Cohen, Columbia, South Carolina

What a change now greets us! The Government is aroused, the dead North is alive, and its divided people united . . . The cry now is for war, vigorous war, war to the bitter end, and war till the traitors are effectually and permanently put down.

Frederick Douglass, after the firing on Fort Sumter,
Douglass' Monthly, May 1861

Now when bricks begin to fly about violently by tons' weight at a time, which is the case when they come in contact with 15-inch shells, they make themselves very unpleasant to those who have trusted to them for protection. This was conclusively shown at Fort Sumter.

Austrian captain Fitzgerald Ross, 1865

We shall be in one of the bloodiest civil wars that history has recorded.

Alexander Stephens, vice-president of the Confederacy,
after the firing on Fort Sumter

Part II.
Fighting the War

✯ ✯ ✯

Union general Ulysses S. Grant and his staff

Broadside, 1862

Enlistment, Conscription, Impressment, and Desertion

Enlistment

How many? We're all a-coming.

Reply of the first soldiers from Massachusetts,
when asked how many volunteers their state
was sending to the war, April 1861

"Who, who, who, and who,
And who goes with you to the war?"
"Ten thousand brave lads, and if they should stay here,
The girls would cry shame, and they'd volunteer."

"The Why and the Wherefore," Union enlistment song

Every soldier, nearly, had a servant with him, and a whole lot of spoons and forks, so as to live comfortably and elegantly in camp, and finally to make a splurge in Washington when they should arrive there, which they expected would be very soon indeed.

Mary A. Ward, in postwar testimony
before Congress, remembering the first troops
to leave from Rome, Georgia

I cannot study, and I wish to join a Horse Company.

Student at the University of Mississippi,
diary entry at the beginning of the war

I know if there is another war this chicken wont be thar when they enlist.

Joe Shields, Confederate private, July 1, 1861

Your requisition is illegal, unconstitutional, revolutionary, inhuman, diabolical, and cannot be complied with.

Claiborne Jackson, governor of Missouri,
in response to Lincoln's call for troops, 1861

I understand that a few days ago the pay Master of Genl. Marshall's command found only five persons in the Kentucky regiments under him who would take pay.

Thomas B. Gordan, Confederate soldier from Kentucky,
letter to his brother, February 11, 1862

I changed my business at one time when I was with my master as a waiter—in the rebel service I was with him Eleven month. I came home with him. I told my son what was going on he with 11 more ran off and joined the Army (the Yankee Army) on St Catherine Island.

> Samuel Elliot, slave, soon after the battle of Williamsburg,
> May 4–5, 1862, and before the Seven Days' battles
> near Chickahominy, June 27–28, 1862

My first duty is to my family, my country is secondary.

> Edwin Fay, Confederate sergeant, June 1862

At the outbreak of the war it was found very difficult to raise infantry in Texas, as no Texan walks a yard if he can help it. Many mounted regiments were therefore organized, and afterward dismounted.

> Sir Arthur James Lyon Fremantle,
> British visitor to Texas, 1863

There are some young men here I think ought to be drummed out of society—the idea of one man staying when his country calls for aid and so anxiously too.

> Kate Foster, Mississippi, June 25, 1863

Never in the toilsome march, nor in the weary watch, nor in the desperate assault, have you rendered a service so decisive in results, as in this last display of the highest qualities of devotion and self-sacrifice which can adorn the warrior-patriot.

> Jefferson Davis, Confederate president, to his soldiers,
> thanking them for continuing to serve,
> though their terms of service (three years) had elapsed,
> February 9, 1864

God has spared me this time. I pray he will spare me to return to you alive and well. I shan't reinlist.

George H. Bates, Union soldier, June 2, 1864

Tallapoosa Thrashers; Baker Fire Eaters; Southern Avengers, Amite Defenders; Butler's Revengers; Bartow Yankee Killers; Chickasaw Desperadoes; Dixie Heroes; Clayton Yellow Jackets; Hornet's Nest Riflemen; Lexington Wild Cats; Green Rough and Readys; Raccoon Roughs; Barbour Yankee Hunters; Southern Rejectors of Old Abe; Cherokee Lincoln Killers; Yankee Terrors; South Florida Bull Dogs.

Some names of volunteer companies of the Confederacy,
The Common Soldier in the Civil War

From my first information of the war my actions feelings and Sympathies have all the time been for the Success and maintainance of the Union Cause & all the time willing and desireous to fight or do any thing else in my power, in that behalf.

Robert Houston, African American soldier

Conscription

In America conscription is unknown and men are induced to enlist by boun-ties. The notions and habits of the people . . . are so opposed to compulsory recruitment that I do not think it can ever be sanctioned by their laws.

Alexis de Tocqueville, French aristocrat who visited
the United States in 1831

I was a ploughboy in the field,
A gawky, lazy dodger,
When came the conscript officer
And took me for a sodger.
He put a musket in my hand,

And showed me how to fire it;
I marched and counter-marched all day;
Lord, how I did admire it!

"The Valiant Conscript,"
sung to the tune of "Yankee Doodle"

I say emphatically, Kentucky will furnish no troops for the wicked purpose of subduing her sister Southern states.

Beriah Magoffin, governor of Kentucky,
in response to Lincoln's call for troops, 1861

Whenever men are forced to fight they take no personal interest in it . . . My private opinion is that our Confederacy is gone, or will go soon.

Charles Moore, Confederate soldier from South Carolina,
on the Conscription Act, April 1862

One of the most surprising results of the conscription was the amount of disease disclosed among men between "eighteen and forty-five" in districts where quotas could not be raised by volunteering.

David Ross Locke, humorist, August 6, 1862

I do not think it is right for me to go through the hardships of camp life and the danger of Battle and others living at home enjoying life because they have a few Negroes.

James Skelton, Confederate soldier,
on the provision in the Conscription Act that exempted
planters owning 20 or more slaves, February 11, 1863

We're coming, Father Abraham, three hundred thousand more
We leave our homes and firesides with bleeding hearts and sore

Since poverty has been our crime, we bow to thy decree;
We are the poor and have no wealth to purchase liberty.

"Song of the Conscripts," in response to a provision
of the 1863 Conscription Act that allowed one
to pay $300 or buy a substitute to avoid the draft

I still cannot help feeling it as a stain, a cause for blushing, that he should
have a substitute.

Sarah Wadley, of her brother Willie's avoidance
of military service

The principle cause of all this discontent was the provision that by paying
three hundred dollars any man could avoid serving if drafted, thus obliging all
who could not beg, borrow, or steal this sum to go to the war. This is exceed-
ingly unjust. The laboring classes say that they are sold for three hundred dollars, whilst they pay one thousand dollars for Negroes.

Maria Lydig Daly, on the New York City draft riots,
Diary of a Union Lady 1861–1865, July 14, 1863

I think the act tyrannical but am satisfied it is the speediest way to put an end
to the war.

Edwin H. Fay, Confederate soldier, on the draft

You who do not wish to be soldiers, do not like this law. This is natural; nor
does it imply want of patriotism. Nothing can be so just, and necessary, as to
make us like it, if it is disagreeable to us.

Abraham Lincoln, on the draft, September 1863

Your people—the Friends—have had, and are having, a very great trial. On principle, and faith, opposed to both war and oppression, they can only practically

oppose oppression by war. In this hard dilemma, some have chosen one horn and
some the other. For those appealing to me on conscientious grounds, I have
done, and shall do, the best I could and can, in my own conscience, under my
oath to the law.

Abraham Lincoln, letter to Eliza Gurney,
wife of a prominent anti-slavery and anti-war
English Quaker, September 4, 1864

"We'll pray for the Conscript with frown on his brow,
To fight for his country, he won't take the vow;
May bad luck and bad fortune him always attend":
"And die with dishonour"—said the Soldier's Amen.

"The Soldier's Amen," a war song

Impressment

To ride up to a man's door, whose hospitable kindness makes you feel welcome & tell him, in the presence of his faithful & loving wife & sunny-faced
children, that he must be ready in 10 minutes to go with you . . . this is indeed
a sad and unpleasant task.

Leonidas L. Polk, Confederate lieutenant
from North Carolina, 1863

Your [politeness,] [petitioners] desire to make known to you that they and
there brothern to the President of the United States are undiscriminately
inpressed by the authorities to labor upon the Public works without compen-
sation that in Consequence of this System of fource labor they have no means
of paying their Rents and otherwise Providing for ther families.

Letter from Robert Henry and other impressed workers
from Beaufort, North Carolina, to Major General B. F. Butler,
November 20, 1863

Complaint is made to me that you are forcing Negroes into the Military service, and even torturing them—riding them on rails and the like—to extort their consent. I hope this may be a mistake.

Abraham Lincoln,
letter to Lieutenant Colonel John Glenn, February 7, 1865

[L]ast fall a large number of we men was Conscript and sent up to the front and all of them has never return Some Got Kill Some died and When they taken them they treated us mean and our owners ever did they taken us just like we had been dum beast.

A letter from African American men in a camp on
Roanoke Island, North Carolina, March 9, 1865

We the soldiers of the 36 U. S. Col[ored] Reg Humbly petition you to alter the Affairs at Roanoke Island.

Richard Etheredge and William Benson,
in a letter to General Oliver O. Howard

We want to know from the Secretary of War has the Rev Chaplain James which is our superintendent of negros affairs has any wright to take our boy Children from us and from the School and Send them to newbern to work to pay for they ration without they parent Consint.

Letter from African American families
whose sons were impressed

I asked the officer for pay when they commenced takeing it It was Lieut Hadlock He consulted with other officers then come back and said part would be paid when we get to Helena and asked how much I expected for it I told him $3.50 the same as others got then he gave me a receipt for it, At Helena he said I must wait for the Pay Master to come Then when I enlisted he was not permitted to pay must wait till mustered out take it with Bounty money After I was mustered out I made unsuccessful attempts for pay till finally the receipt was worne out and lost.

Robert Houston, impressed African American soldier

Desertion

Officers state that they see letters from wives received by privates in which their families plead for them to come home at every hazard . . . women selling their last extra dress for food.

Augusta Jane Evans, Mobile, December 20, 1862

He liked the war, but didn't like to do his share.

Edmund Patterson, Confederate soldier,
of a conscript who deserted, March 1863

It take one half of the men to keep the other half from running away.

James Bracy, Confederate soldier, May 11, 1863

Must I shoot a simple-minded soldier boy who deserts, while I must not touch a hair of a wiley agitator who induces him to desert? . . . I think that in such a case, to silence the agitator, and save the boy, is not only constitutional, but a great mercy.

Abraham Lincoln, letter to Albany Democrat Erastus Corning,
defending the banishment of Clement L. Vallandigham,
June 12, 1863

There are few crimes in the sight of either God or man, that are more wicked and detestable than desertion.

John Paris, chaplain, sermon given on the occasion
of the hanging of 22 Confederate deserters,
February 1864

The Deserters were marched around where their graves were dug. Their coffins which was mearly rough board boxes were plased over their graves and each one was seated on their own coffins. There each one could see his final resting place.

Soldier describing the execution of several deserters

One man told me that he had remained in the trenches till a conscript who had lately arrived from his neighborhood told him that his family was starving.

Cornelia McDonald, Virginia,
on Southern deserters at the end of the war

Money you have expended without limits and blood poured out like water. Defeat, debt, taxation, and sepulchers—these are your only trophies.

Clement L. Vallandigham, Ohio congressman,
who called on Union soldiers to desert
and avoid conscription; he was later convicted
of treason and banished to the Confederate lines

The men seem to think desertion is no crime and hence never shoot a deserter when he goes over—they always shoot but never hit.

Luther Rice Mills, Confederate soldier,
on life under siege in Petersburg, Summer 1864

To fill up the Army is like undertaking to shovel fleas. You take up a shovelful but before you can dump them anywhere they are gone.

Abraham Lincoln, to White House visitors,
quoted by Mary A. Livermore, *My Story of the War*

General, there are already too many weeping widows in the United States. For God's sake, don't ask me to add to the number, for I won't do it.

Abraham Lincoln, to a Union officer
who wanted the president to sign warrants
of execution for 24 deserters

President of the Confederate States of America

Jefferson Davis

The man and the hour have met.

William L. Yancey, Alabama secessionist,
introducing Jefferson Davis to the Confederate
Convention, Montgomery, February 4, 1861

We are fighting for independence, and that, or extermination, we will have.

Jefferson Davis, president of the Confederate States of America

He was a warm friend and a bitter enemy . . . He was a regular bull-dog when he formed an opinion, for he would never let go.

> A clerk under Jefferson Davis when he served
> as U.S. president Franklin Pierce's secretary of war

Davis is venal and corrupt, and the Confederate Congress is no better.

> Thomas J. Withers, Confederate congressman
> from South Carolina, May 1861

Mr. Davis is a man of slight, sinewy figure, rather over the middle height, and of erect, soldierlike bearing. His is about fifty-five years of age; his features are regular and well-defined, but the face is thin and marked on cheek and brow with many wrinkles, and is rather careworn and haggard.

> William Howard Russell,
> correspondent to the *London Times*, May 7, 1861

I have learned that cordial co-operation between officers is not vital to success.

> Jefferson Davis,
> on the infighting among his Western generals

Mr. Davis had an exalted opinion of his own military genius.

> Ulysses S. Grant, Union general

We have made a great mistake in the choice of President.

> Robert Smith,
> Confederate congressman from Alabama, December 1861

Jeff Davis rode a dapple gray,
Lincoln rode a mule,

Jeff Davis is a gentleman,
And Lincoln is a fool.

Verse from a Confederate song

He lacks system, is very slow, does not discriminate between important and unimportant matter, has no practical knowledge of the workings of our military system in the field.

George W. Randolph,
Confederate secretary of war, letter to his brother,
having resigned from his post, November 1862

It is not only honorable to our women to weave and wear their dresses, but really homespun is becoming to them.

Jefferson Davis, encouraging white Southern women
to revive home production in order to assist the
lagging Confederate economy, 1862

Jefferson Davis is not only a dishonest man, but a liar.

Barnwell Rhett, Confederate congressman
from South Carolina, April 15, 1864

The one was an unsettled, shifting, vulgar, rollicking man—the other serious, grave, dignified, and determined. The one was plebeian by nature—the other a nobleman.

"Abraham Lincoln and Jefferson Davis: A Comparison"
(in which Davis fares the better), The Land We Love, 1868

The South did not fall crushed by the mere weight of the North; but it was nibbled away at all sides and ends, because its executive head never gathered and wielded its great strength.

Pierre Beauregard, Confederate general,
in Battles and Leaders of the Civil War, 1884-87

My only apology for troubling you with this communication arises from the fact that I regard you as "the Father of the people" over whom God has called you to preside, and believe therefore that even amid the engrossing and perplexing cares of public business, there is sympathy in your great and noble heart for individual suffering, and a just regard for private claims.

Diana Johnson, a young war widow, Mobile,
requesting government employment and assistance

Now when he saw the game was up,
He started for the woods,
His handbox hung upon his arm
Quite full of fancy goods;
Said Jeff, "They'll never take me now,
I'm sure I'll not be seen.
They'd never think to look for me
Beneath my crinoline."

"Jeff in Petticoats," a song elaborating on the rumor
Jefferson Davis was wearing a dress when captured

Altho' he tried to keep us all slaves . . . some of us well know of many kindness he shown his slaves on his plantation.

Group of Mississippi freedmen,
on why they pushed for Davis's release from prison

Echoes

A widespread desire among northern men to make a mockery of southern manhood.

Nina Silber, historian, on the rumors that Davis
was attempting to escape disguised in a dress
at the time of his capture, 1992

John Hunt Morgan, Nathan Bedford Forrest, Leonidas Polk, Albert Sidney Johnston, John Brown Gordon, Wade Hampton, Richard Stoddert Ewell, James Ewell Brown "Jeb" Stuart, Jefferson Davis, Pierre Gustave Toutant Beauregard, Robert Edward Lee, Sterling Pierce, Joseph Eggleston Johnston, Ambrose Powell Hill, Thomas Jonathan "Stonewall" Jackson, Braxton Bragg

Confederate Military Leaders

Pierre Gustave Toutant Beauregard

Oh! the North was evil-starred, when she met thee, Beauregard!

Popular toast to the general,
recorded by T. C. DeLeon, 1907

His aloofness made a favorable impression. It was thought that he disliked demonstrations of worship and that he wished to devote all his time in planning destruction for the Yankees.

T. Harry Williams, *Beauregard, Napoleon in Gray*, 1955

His strategy was mostly in a vast dream world, where nonexistent armies moved across impossible terrain, without having to eat, and never running out of ammunition.

John Elting, historian at the U.S. Military Academy, 1965

Braxton Bragg

Bragg is beyond doubt the best disciplinarian in the South. When he took command at Corinth, the army was little better than a mob.

John Buie, Confederate soldier,
September 30, 1862

He loved to crush the spirit of his men. The more of a hangdog look they had about them the better was General Bragg pleased. Not a single soldier in the whole army ever loved or respected him.

Confederate soldier

Nathan Bedford Forrest

I must express my distaste to being commanded by a man having no pretension to gentility—a negro trader, gambler—an ambitious man, careless of the lives of his men so long as preferment be *en prospectu*. Forrest may be & no doubt is, the best Cav officer in the West, but I object to a tyrannical, hotheaded vulgarian's commanding me.

Harry St. John Dixon, Confederate soldier, 1864

Thomas J. "Stonewall" Jackson

I seem to have a more perfect command of my facul[ties in the midst of fighting.

Stonewall Jackson

Jackson is profoundly and, some say, fanatically religious, with a precise regard for discipline and army regulations. A man he is of contracts so complete that he appears one day a Presbyterian deacon who delights in a theological discussion and, the next reincarnated Joshua. He lives by the new testament and fights by the old.

Douglas Southall Freeman, writer

He was the true type of all great soldiers. He did not value human life where he had an object to accomplish. He could order men to their death as a matter of course.

Mary Chesnut

All admire his genius and great deeds; no one could love the man for himself. He seems to be cut off from his fellow-man and to commune with his own spirits only, or with spirits of which we wot not.

Confederate officer, August 1862

Let us cross the river, and rest in the shade of the trees.

Stonewall Jackson, dying words, May 10, 1863

There was something so daring a[nd] Noble in his way of fighting that made his enemys love him . . . Those men that praise him and his daring would not hesitate a moment if they had the Chance to send a Ball through his heart.

Hugh Roden, Union soldier,
of the late Stonewall Jackson, May 1863

He has lost his left arm, but I have lost my right.

> Robert E. Lee, Confederate general,
> on hearing of Stonewall Jackson's death
> following the Battle of Chancellorsville,
> May 4, 1863, in which he lost his left arm

He followed no star, he sought no throne, he asked no earthly guerdon, was guided by no selfish consideration, and lured by no vulgar ambition. Duty, and duty alone, was the principle of his conduct.

> *Southern Illustrated News*,
> of Stonewall Jackson, on the occasion of his death
> after the Battle of Chancellorsville, May 4, 1863

Stonewall Jackson was a great general, a brave soldier, a noble Christian, and a pure man. May God throw these great virtues against the sins of the secessionist, the advocate of a great national crime.

> John W. Forney, editor of the *Washington Chronicle*

It is not fair to compare me with General Lee and General Jackson. The world has produced few such men as they were and I am certainly not one of them.

> Jubal Early, former Confederate general, 1871

Tobacco Jackson never used. Whiskey he avoided because he thought he might come to like it.

> Douglass Freeman, historian, 1961

To Jackson a man who fell out from exhaustion on a march, or a man who could not keep up because his feet hurt, lacked patriotism.

> Colonel Red Reeder, *The Southern Generals*, 1965

He tried to kill as many of the enemy as possible, and he did not shrink from getting his own men killed doing it. Jackson did not go through the Civil War's often-described transition from notions of chivalric gallantry to brutal attrition. For him the war was always earnest, massed, lethal.

Charles Royster, *The Destructive War*, 1991

Albert Sydney Johnston

If Sidney Johnston is not a general, I have none to give you.

Jefferson Davis, Confederate president,
defending General A. S. Johnston
after he surrendered two forts in the Midwest

Robert Edward Lee

He is about five feet ten inches high, was eminently handsome in his youth, is still one of the finest looking men in the army, rides like a knight of the old crusading days, is indefatigable in business, and bears fatigue like a man of iron.

On Robert E. Lee in *The War and Its Heroes*,
booklet published in Richmond, 1864

You will, however, learn before this reaches you that our success at Gettysburg was not so great as reported—in fact, that we failed to drive the enemy from his position, and that our army withdrew to the Potomac. Had the river not unexpectedly risen, all would have been well with us; but God, in His all-wise providence, willed otherwise, and our communications have been interrupted and almost cut off.

Robert E. Lee, in a letter to his family,
in *Recollections and Letters of General Robert E. Lee*

In the old army he was believed by all officers, almost without exception to be, by many degrees, the most accomplished soldier in the whole army. His superiority, indeed, was so incontestable, that it excited no jealousy whatever in any quarter.

The War and Its Heroes,
booklet published in Richmond, 1864

I have been up to see Congress and they do not seem to be able to do anything except to eat peanuts and chew tobacco, while my army is starving.

Robert E. Lee

You are the country to these men. They fought for you.

Henry Wise, Confederate general, to Robert E. Lee,
shortly before the surrender at Appomattox

Aren't you ashamed to give Lee the privilege of being a President of a college? Satan wouldn't have him to open the door for fresh arrivals, and you have pardoned him.

Southern Unionist, letter to U.S. president Andrew Johnson,
October 1, 1865

It would be better for every officer, including myself, to die, than Robert E. Lee.

Winfield Scott, U.S. general, after the Mexican War

Lee could not be beaten. Overpowered . . . he might be, but never defeated.

John Gordon, Confederate general,
at a meeting of veterans of the Army of Northern Virginia,
November 1870, weeks after Lee's death

A leader of men in war and peace, a champion of principles, a humanitarian, a man who devoted his entire life to the benefit of others without regard to himself. Time after time, he was offered opportunities to gain fame and wealth, but neither factor influenced his decision to take a course of action he conscientiously believed to be right.

Woodrow Wilson, 28th president of the United States

It took five generations of clean living and wise mating to produce such a man.

Douglas Freeman, 1934

[Robert E. Lee] became a God figure for Virginians, a saint for the white Protestant South, and a hero for the nation.

Thomas L. Connelly, *The Marble Man*, 1977

Major John Singleton Mosby

The face of this person is tanned, beardless, youthful-looking and pleasant. He has white and regular teeth, which his habitual smile reveals. His piercing eyes flash out from beneath his brown hat, with its golden cord, and he reins in his horse with the ease of a practiced rider. A plain soldier, low and slight in stature, ready to talk, to laugh, to ride, to oblige you in any way—such was Mosby, in outward appearance. Nature had given no sign but the restless, roving, flashing eye, that there was much worth considering beneath.

John Esten Cooke, *Wearing the Gray*

There was nobody but soldiers on this train, but, if there had been women and children, too, it would have been all the same to me . . . [I] did not understand that it hurts women and children to be killed any more than it hurts men.

John Mosby, on one of the trains he shelled

None know his daring enterprise and dashing heroism, better than those foul invaders, though strangers themselves to such noble traits.

Jeb Stuart, Confederate general,
March 12, 1863

"Who is that?" growled the sleepy brigadier.
"Get up quick, I want you," responded the major.
"Do you know who I am," cried the brigadier, sitting up in bed, with a scowl. "I will have you arrested sir."
"Do you know who I am?" retorted the major, shortly.
"Who are you?"
"Did you ever hear of Mosby?"
"Yes! Tell me, have you caught the —— rascal?"
"No; but he has caught you!" And the major chuckled.

John Esten Cooke,
Southern Illustrated News, on Major John Mosby's
capture of Brigadier-General Stoughton, Spring 1863

He has been the chief actor in so many raids, encounters and adventures, that his memoirs, if he committed them to paper, would be regarded as the efforts of his fancy.

The War and Its Heroes, 1864

When any of Mosby's men are caught, hang them without trial.

Ulysses S. Grant, Union general

James Ewell Brown "Jeb" Stuart

How well I remember Stuart as he looked that day! He wore a fine, new uniform, brilliant with gold lace, buff gauntlets reaching to his elbows, and a canary-colored silk sash with tassled ends. His hat, a soft, broad brimmed felt, was caught up at the side with a gold star and carried a sweeping plume; his high, patent-leather cavalry boots were trimmed with gold . . . And how happy he was—how full of faith in the Confederacy and himself.

Myrta Lockett Avery,
of Confederate general Jeb Stuart at a grand review,
A Virginia Girl in the Civil War 1861-1865

Our Jeb Stuart is never tired. You could wake him with a message any time of night and he's awake on the instant.

Confederate soldier in Barry Hannah's short story,
"Knowing He Was Not My Kind Yet I Followed," 1978

Lincoln and McClellan at Antietam

Union Military Leaders

The Confederacy had no more effective foes than [Lincoln, Grant, and Sherman.] Lincoln had led the North into war, had held firmly to its task, and had refused to hear any talk of peace that was not based on the extinction of the Confederate Government. Grant seemed to be the very incarnation of the remorseless killer, and Sherman was destruction's own self, his trail across the South a band of ruin sixty miles wide. Yet it was these three who were most determined that vindictiveness and hatred must not control the future.

Bruce Catton,
The Army of the Potomac: A Stillness at Appomattox

Benjamin Franklin Butler

As I looked on their bronzed faces upturned in the shining sun to heaven as if in mute appeal against the wrongs of the country for which they had given their lives . . . feeling I had wronged them in the past . . . I swore to myself a solemn oath . . . to defend the rights of these men who had given their blood for me and my country.

Benjamin Butler, recalling 500 black soldiers
who died on the shore of the James River

As the officers and soldiers of the United States have been subject to repeated insults from the women (calling themselves ladies) of New Orleans, in return for the most scrupulous non-interference and courtesy on our part, it is ordered that hereafter when any female shall, by word, gesture, or movement, insult or show contempt for any officer or soldier of the United States, she shall be regarded and held liable to be treated as a woman of the town plying her trade.

Benjamin Butler,
General Orders No. 28, May 15, 1862

If the Federal Government cannot pass laws to protect the rights, liberty, and lives of citizens of the United States in the States, why were guarantees of those fundamental rights out in the constitution at all?

Benjamin Butler, on the Enforcement Acts
to counteract Ku Klux Klan terrorism, 1870

B eastly by instinct, a tyrant and sot,
U gly and venomous—on mankind a blot—
T hief, liar, and scoundrel, in highest degree,
L et Yankeedom boast of such heroes as thee!
E very woman and child will for ages to come
R emember thee, monster—thou vilest of scum!

Confederate soldier

George Cooke

He will regret it but once, and that will be continually.

Jeb Stuart, Confederate general,
on the decision of his father-in-law,
Union general George Cooke, to stay in the Union army

Ulysses S. Grant

No terms except unconditional and immediate surrender can be accepted.

Grant, to the defeated Confederate general
at Fort Donelson, thus gaining the nickname
Unconditional Surrender Grant

Not a great man except morally; not an original or brilliant man, but sincere, thoughtful, deep and gifted with courage that never failed.

Charles Dana, U.S. under secretary of war

Grant is played out with me[.] [W]e were strong enough to drive the rebells if we wer managed right, but no he would bring us up in a Single line when the rebels were 6 or 8 deep and any fool would know we could not stand then.

Thomas N. Lewis, Union private,
on the Battle of Shiloh, April 10, 1862

General Grant, entrusted with our greatest army, is a jackass in the original package. He is a poor drunken imbecile. He is a poor stick sober, and he is most of the time more than half-drunk, and much of the time idiotically drunk . . . Grant will fail miserably, hopelessly, eternally.

Marat Halstead, editor of the Cincinnati Commercial,
letter to his friend Salmon P. Chase,
secretary of the treasury

By the way, can you tell me where he gets his whiskey? He has given us successes and if his whiskey does it, I should like to send a barrel of the same brand to every general in the field.

Abraham Lincoln, responding to complaints
about Grant's drinking habits

Grant is my man, and I am his the rest of the war!

Abraham Lincoln,
after the capture of Vicksburg, July 4, 1863

She expressed her pleasure at meeting him, yet I could see it was not quite
easy on either side . . . Grant was reticent yet kindly . . . [When] the thin ice
broke [and] words flowed freely on both sides—she telling him how his tasks
and trials were appreciated, and how much faith was placed in his upright
doing of duty to the oppressed, and he quietly, yet with much feeling,
expressing the hope that he might be wise and firm and never forget the
inalienable rights of all.

Giles Stebbins, recounting Sojourner Truth's visit
with Grant, 1870

Joseph Hooker

I believe you to be a brave and a skillful soldier, which, of course, I like. I also
believe you do not mix politics with your profession, in which you are right.
You have confidence in yourself . . . you are ambitious, which, within reasonable
bounds, does good rather than harm. But I think that during Gen. Burnside's
command of the Army, you have taken counsel of your ambition, and thwarted
him as much as you could, in which you did a great wrong to your country.

I have heard . . . of your recently saying that both the Army and the
Government needed a Dictator. Of course it was not for this, but in spite of it,
that I have given you the command. Only those generals who gain successes,
can set up dictators. What I now ask of you is military success, and I will risk
the dictatorship.

Abraham Lincoln,
letter to General Joseph Hooker, January 26, 1863

George Brinton McClellan

I find myself in a new and strange position here. President, Gen. Scott, and all deferring to me. By some strange operation of magic, I seem to have become the power of the land.

George McClellan,
letter to his wife on receiving command of
the Federal Division of the Potomac, July 1861

If he had a million men he would swear the enemy has two millions, and then he would sit down in the mud and yell for three.

Edwin M. Stanton, U.S. secretary of war

It is called the Army of the Potomac, but it is only McClellan's bodyguard . . . If McClellan is not using the army, I should like to borrow it for a while.

Abraham Lincoln,
unsent note regarding General McClellan, April 9, 1862

General McClellan, if I understand you correctly, before you strike at the Rebels, you want to be sure of plenty of room so you can run in case they strike back.

Zachariah Chandler, senator from Michigan
and member of the Joint Committee on the
Conduct of the War, questioning General George McClellan
on why he did not march against the enemy, 1862

McClellan's vice . . . was always waiting to have everything just as he wanted before he would attack, and before he could get things arranged as he wanted them, the enemy pounced on him.

George Meade, Union general

I feel quite sure that this country will yet come to the conclusion that Geo. B. McClellan is either a cold-blooded Traitor, or that he is an unmitigated military Imposter. He has shown no heart in his conduct, except when doing something directly in favor of the rebels, such as guarding their persons and property and offering his services to suppress with an iron hand any attempt on the part of the slaves against their rebel masters.

Frederick Douglass, July 4, 1862

The effect of this man's presence upon the Army of the Potomac—in sunshine or in rain, in darkness or in daylight, in victory or defeat—was electrical, and too wonderful to make it worthwile attempting to give a reason for it.

Witness of General McClellan's return
to the command of the army, September 1862

He went beyond the formal military salute, and gave his cap a little twirl, which with his bow and smile seemed to carry a little of personal good fellowship even to the humblest private soldier . . . It was very plain that these little attentions to the troops took well, and had no small influence in establishing a sort of comradeship between him and them.

Union officer

I have just read your despatch about sore tongued and fatiegued horses. Will you pardon me for asking what the horses of your army have done since the battle of Antietam that fatigue anything?

Abraham Lincoln,
letter to General McClellan, October 24, 1862

He has got an eye like a hawk. I looked him right in the eye and he done the same by me.

Union recruit from Massachusetts

Alas, for my poor country! I know in my inmost heart she never had a truer servant.

> George McClellan,
> on being removed from command, November 1862

There's little McClellan, of our army the boast,
He never complained when removed from his post—
The brave deeds he done bring their own recompense,
He won't be forgotten a hundred years hence.

> "One Hundred Years Hence"

He believed beyond any doubt that his Confederate enemies faced him with forces substantially greater than his own. He believed with equal conviction that enemies at the head of his own government conspired to see him and his army defeated so as to carry out their traitorous purposes. He believed himself to be God's chosen instrument for saving the Union. When he lost the courage to fight, as he did in every battle, he believed he was preserving his army to fight the next time on another and better day.

> Stephen W. Sears,
> *The Young Napoleon*, 1988

George Gordon Meade

Well, I've been tried and condemned without a hearing, and I suppose I shall have to go to execution.

> George Meade, on being given the command of the
> Army of the Potomac, June 27, 1863

Philip Henry Sheridan

A cavalryman should be at least six feet four high, but I have changed my mind—five feet four will do in a pinch.

> Abraham Lincoln

William Tecumseh Sherman

The Attila of the American continent.

> Jefferson Davis, Confederate president

The government of the United States may now safely proceed on the proper rule that all in the South are enemies of all in the North.

> William T. Sherman, letter to Salmon P. Chase,
> secretary of the treasury, August 1862

I begin to regard the death and mangling of a couple thousand men as a small affair, a kind of morning dash.

> William T. Sherman, June 30, 1864

He took the little child of my friend in his arms, and patted her rosy cheeks, calling her a "poor little exile," and saying he was sorry to have to drive her away from her comfortable home, but that war was a cruel, and inexorable thing, and its necessities compelled him to do many things, which he heartily regretted.

> George McDonnell, of General Sherman's exchange
> with some citizens of Atlanta, November 4, 1864

I cannot feel kindly toward Gen. Sherman. He was a monster and I want the whole world to know it.

> Elizabeth Avery Meriwether,
> more than 50 years after Appomattox

Negro recruits marching up Beekman Street, New York City, from the Pictorial War Record

African American Soldiers

The Debate

In the early days you scorned them,
And with many a flip and flout,
Said, "these battles are the white man's
And the whites will fight them out."

Paul Laurence Dunbar (1872–1906), "The Colored Soldiers"

We want you damned niggers to keep out of this; this is a white man's war.

Policeman to the owner of a building in Cincinnati
turned into a recruiting station for a company of
African American "Home Guards," 1861

The whites knew that we were willing to fight, and therefore there was no need of laying ourselves liable to insult, simply for the privilege of saying so.

Argument of some speakers at a meeting of
African Americans in New York City, on a proposed resolution
to offer their services to defend the state, May 1, 1861

We don't want to fight side and side with the nigger. We think we are too superior a race for that.

Corporal Felix Brannigan, 74th New York Regiment

Some tell me 'tis a burnin' shame
To make the naygers fight,
And that the trade of bein' kilt
Belongs but to the white.
But as for me, upon my soul!
So liberal are we here,
I'll let Sambo be shot instead of myself
On ev'ry day in the year.

"Sambo's Right to Be Kilt," a Union soldier song

We earnestly recommend that the colored citizens stand prepared, so that when officially solicited by the Government, we may render such service as only men can render, who know how precious Liberty is.

Leaders of the African Americans of Philadelphia,
Christian Recorder, May 4, 1861

If the colored people, under all the social and legal disabilities by which they are environed, are ever ready to defend the government that despoils them of their rights, it may be concluded that it is quite safe to oppress them.

African American from Chillicothe, Ohio,
Pine and Palm, May 25, 1861

We, the members of the first and only equipped military Company, have more knowledge of our duty, and also more dignity, than to offer our services to a Government, when knowing at the same time, that the laws call for none but white men to do military duty . . . I, as the Captain, in behalf of the Company, am resolved never to offer or give service, except it be on equality with all other men.

Henry Cropper, African American from Philadelphia,
Pine and Palm, May 25, 1861

The national edifice is on fire. Every man who can carry a bucket of water, or remove a brick, is wanted; but those who have the care of the building, having a profound respect for the feeling of the national burglars who set the building on fire, are determined that the flames shall only be extinguished by Indo-Caucasian hands, and to have the building burnt rather than save it by means of any other. Such is the pride, the stupid prejudice and folly that rules the hour.

Frederick Douglass, on the Union's refusal to enlist
African Americans, *Douglass' Monthly*, September 1861

What rights have we in the free States? We have the "right to life, liberty and the pursuit of happiness." We have the right to labor, and are secured in the fruits of our labor; we have the right to our wives and our little ones . . . Are these rights worth having? If they are then they are worth defending with all our might, and at any cost. It is illogical, unpatriotic, nay mean and unmanly in us to shrink from the defense of these great rights and privileges.

Anglo-African, New York City weekly, September 14, 1861

No regiments of black troops should leave their bodies to rot upon the battle-field beneath a Southern sun, to conquer a peace based on the perpetuity of human bondage.

African American with the initials R.H.V.,
letter to the *Anglo-African*, September 28, 1861

It being their fight I assure you they are welcome to it, so far as I am concerned.

William H. Parham, African American schoolteacher
from Cincinnati, letter to a friend, October 12, 1861

From all I have observed of the negro he is much too averse to work, too timid to make a good soldier, and has got it into his head that liberty means doing nothing.

Frances Dallam Peter, slaveowner and Union supporter,
from Lexington, Kentucky, on enlisting black soldiers

If we could make them soldiers, the condition of the soldier being socially equal to any other in society, we could make them officers, perhaps to command white men.

Senator M. T. Hunter,
on why having African American soldiers would be
an admission that slavery has been unjust all along

I have seen men drilled among our sturdy colored men of the rural districts of Pennsylvania and New Jersey, in the regular African Zouave Drill, that would make the hearts of secession traitors, or prejudiced northern Yankees, quake and tremble for fear.

Alfred M. Green, Philadelphia schoolteacher,
Anglo-African, October 14, 1861

[Our fathers] put confidence in the word of the whites only to feel the dagger of slavery driven still deeper into the heart throbbing with emotions of joy for freedom. We are not going to re-enact that trajedy.

African American from Troy, New York,
letter to the *Anglo-African*, October 19, 1861

I have observed with much indignation and shame, their willingness to take up arms in defence of this unholy, ill-begotten, would-be Republican government, that summons all its skill, energy, and might, of money, men, and false philosophy that a corrupt nation can bring to bear, to support, extend, and perpetuate that vilest of all vile systems, American slavery.

Wesley W. Tate, African American, Denver,
letter to the editor of the *Pine and Palm*, November 23, 1861

Such is their servility, that fifty of their Masters would put to flight a Reg. of them. Poor helpless Creatures, raised as a farmer Raises Stock, alowed a Peck of Corn a week for subsistence . . . & with an abject servility which is painful, it would be folly to employ them on either side.

John Buchanan, Union soldier,
on enlisting blacks for combat service

I know they says dese tings but dey lies. Our masters may talk now all dey choose; but one tings sartin, dey don't dare to try us. Jess put de guns into our hans, and you'll soon see dat we not only knows how to shoot, but who to shoot.

Tom, in response to the suggestion
that African American slaves love their masters
so much they would not be able to fight Southerners

I think it is time to take the Negroes & let them die & be killed off instead of our best men.

Ann Cotton, Northerner, March 3, 1863

Why should we be alarmed at their threat of hanging us; do we intend to become their prisoners?

Anglo-African, trying to persuade Northern blacks
to enlist, quoted in *Douglass' Monthly*, March 1863

Facts are beginning to dispel prejudices. Enemies of the negro race, who have persistently denied the capacity and doubted the courage of the Blacks, are unanswerably confuted by the good conduct and gallant deeds of the men whom they persecuted and slander.

New York Tribune, March 28, 1863

It is astonishing to me that our people do not pass laws to form regiments of blacks. The Yankees are fighting low foreigners against the best of our people, whereas were we to fight our Negroes they would be a fair offset.

Richard S. Ewell, Confederate general

If slaves will make good soldiers, our whole theory of slavery is wrong.

Howell Cobb, secessionist, Georgia,
on enlisting blacks into the Confederate army, July 1863

Once let the black man get upon his person the brass letters, U.S., let him get an eagle on his button, and a musket on his shoulder and bullets in his pocket, and there is no power on earth which can deny that he has earned the right to citizenship in the United States.

Frederick Douglass, *Douglass' Monthly*, August 1863

You say you will not fight to free negroes. Some of them seem willing to fight for you.

Abraham Lincoln, public letter
reproving Northern opponents of emancipation
and African American troops, August 26, 1863

I take a woman's view of the subject but it does seem strangely inconsistent the idea of our offering to a Negro the rich boon—the priceless reward of freedom to aid us in keeping in bondage a large portion of his brethren when by joining the Yankees he will instantly gain the very reward which Mr. Davis offers to him after a certain amount of labor rendered and danger incurred.

Ella Gertrude Clanton Thomas,
on Jefferson Davis's proposal to enlist blacks
in the Confederate army, November 17, 1864

African Americans Fighting for the North

Young men of military experience, of firm Anti-slavery principles, ambitious, superior to the vulgar contempt of color, and having faith in the capacity of colored men for military service.

John A. Andrew, governor of Massachusetts,
listing the qualities he wanted in (white)
officers of black regiments

The bare sight of 50,000 armed and drilled black soldiers upon the banks of the Mississippi would end the rebellion at once.

Abraham Lincoln, letter to Andrew Johnson,
war governor of Tennessee, March 26, 1863

I know as fully as anyone can know the opinions of others, that some of the commanders of our armies in the field, who have given us our most important successes, believe that the emancipation policy and the use of colored troops constitute the heaviest blow yet dealt to the rebellion, and that at least one of these important successes could not have been achieved when it was but for the aid of black soldiers . . .

Abraham Lincoln, in response to the bravery of
ex-slave regiments at Port Hudson
and Milliken's Bend, Spring 1863

This charge was resisted by the negro portion of the enemy's force with considerable obstinacy, while the white or true Yankee portion ran like whipped curs.

Henry McCulloch, Confederate general,
of the attack on Milliken's Bend, June 1863

If we do not fight, we are traitors to our God, traitors to our country, traitors to our race, and traitors to ourselves. Richmond is the place for us, and we mean to go there. Our friend Jeff. Davis, says we shall go there, and we will go; but they won't be glad to see us.

Sayles Bowen, African American,
rallying recruits at a church meeting, June 1863

The average plantation negro was a hard-looking specimen, with about as little of the soldier to be seen in him as there was of the angel in Michel Angelo's block of marble before he has applied his chisel.

Robert Cowden,
white officer of the 59th U.S. Colored Infantry,
recalling recruitment and training in Memphis, June 1863

McClellan went to Richmond with two hundred thousand brave;
He said, "keep back the niggers," and the Union he would save.
Little Mac he had his way—still the Union is in tears—
Now they call for the colored volunteers.

So rally, boys, rally, let us never mind the past;
We had a hard road to travel, but our day is coming fast,
For God is for the right, and we have no need to fear—
The Union must be saved by the colored volunteer.

Song written by a private in the
54th Massachusetts Volunteers,
reported in the *Liberator*, June 1863

I want you to prove yourselves. The eyes of thousands will look on what you do tonight.

Robert Gould Shaw, Union colonel,
commander of the 54th Massachusetts Volunteers,
a black regiment, addressing his troops
before the assault on Fort Wagner, July 18, 1863

Here the flag of this regiment was planted; here General Strong fell mortally wounded; and here the brave, beautiful, and heroic Colonel Shaw was saluted by death and kissed by immortality.

George W. Williams, African American historian,
on the failed assault on Fort Wagner, July 18, 1863,
by the 54th Massachusetts Volunteers, 1888

The old flag never touched the ground.

Sergeant William H. Carney of the 54th
Massachusetts Volunteers, the first African
American soldier to win a Congressional Medal of Honor

The poor benighted wretches thought they were heaping indignities upon his dead body; but the act recoils upon them . . . We can imagine no holier place than where he is.

Robert Gould Shaw's father,
on learning that Confederates tossed his son's body
into a mass grave with the bodies of the black soldiers
who died in the attack on Fort Wagner, July 1863

The next day the 31st several flags of truce were sent from our lines proposing to recover the wounded and bury the dead, the rebels would not allow us to take the wounded negroes who laid strewn over the field [and] constituted the greater part of those who had fallen between the respective Forts of the opposing parties. The whites they allowed us to take.

Samuel Rodman Smith of the 4th Delaware Regiment,
letter to his mother

To sell or enslave any captured person, on account of his color, and for no offence against the laws of war, is a relapse into barbarism and a crime against the civilization of the age. The government of the United States will give the same protection to all its soldiers . . . for every soldier of the United States killed in violation of the laws of war, a rebel soldier shall be executed; and for every one enslaved by the enemy or sold into slavery, a rebel soldier shall be placed at hard labor.

> Abraham Lincoln, order of retaliation, July 30, 1863

We don't know any black men here, they're all soldiers.

> White Union soldier,
> after the assault on Fort Wagner, July 31, 1863

Many old, respectable darkies stood at the street corners, men and women with tears in their eyes as if they saw the redemption of their race afar off but still the beginning of a better state of affairs for them. Though I am very little Negrophilish and would always prefer the commonest white that lives to a Negro, still I could not but feel moved.

> Maria Lydig Daly, on watching the first black regiment
> from New York City march down the street for the front

This, with the emancipation of the negro, is the heavyest blow yet given the Confederacy.

> Ulysses S. Grant, Union general,
> on enlisting African American troops,
> letter to Abraham Lincoln, August 23, 1863

The patient, trusting Descendants of Afric's clime have dyed the ground with blood, in defense of the Union, and Democracy. Men, too, your Excellency, who know in a measure the cruelties of the Iron heel of oppression, which in years gone by, the very Power their blood is now being spilled to maintain ever ground them to the dust.

> James Henry Gooding, 54th Massachusetts Volunteers,
> letter to Abraham Lincoln, September 28, 1863

This year has brought about many changes that at the beginning were or would have been thought impossible. The close of the year finds me a soldier for the cause of my race. May God bless the cause, and enable me in the coming year, to forward it on.

> Christopher Fleetwood, African American soldier
> from Baltimore, diary entry, December 1863

I would sooner stay here . . . than have our Government acede to their demands in regard to the negro soldier . . . Anyone, whatever may be his color, who wears the blue of Uncle Sam is entitled to protection, even if thousands have to be sacrificed in protecting him.

> James Gaunt Derrickson, Union army captain,
> prisoner of war when the Union refused
> a prisoner exchange unless the Confederates treated
> black prisoners according to the rules of war, 1864

General Forrest captured Fort Pillow and about six hundred the most of them was Negroes[,] he didn't [take] any of them prisoners[,] killed every one of them[.] I think that was the best thing he iver done in his life.

> Richard White, Confederate soldier, April 23, 1864

Damn you, you are fighting against your master.

> Rebel soldier to his prisoner, George Shaw,
> an African American private, before he shot him
> in the mouth and threw him in the river,
> reported by Shaw to a congressional committee
> investigating the Fort Pillow massacre of
> African American troops by Confederate soldiers, 1864

I went to see my mistress on furlough, and she was glad to see me. She said, "You remember when you were sick and I had to bring you to the house and nurse you?" and I told her, "Yes'm, I remember." And she said, "And now you are fighting me!" I said, "No'm, I ain't fighting you, I'm fighting to get free."

> Ex-slave and soldier, Tennessee

The river was dyed with the blood of the slaughtered for 200 yards. It is hoped that these facts will demonstrate to the northern people that negro soldiers cannot cope with Southerners.

Nathan Bedford Forrest,
Confederate general and future grand wizard
of the Ku Klux Klan, following the massacre at Fort Pillow

Blood can not restore blood.

Abraham Lincoln,
in a letter to U.S. secretary of war
Edwin M. Stanton, regarding non-retaliation
for the massacre at Fort Pillow, May 17, 1864

Any different policy in regard to the colored man deprives us of his help, and this is more than we can bear. We can not spare the hundred and forty or fifty thousand now serving us as soldiers, seamen, and laborers. This is not a question of sentiment or taste, but of physical force which may be measured and estimated as horse-power and steam-power are measured and estimated. Keep it and you can save the Union. Throw it away, and the Union goes with it.

Abraham Lincoln, September 1864

When I was home I used to run down colored troops as bad as any one, but one month in Virginia has entirely cured me of that as they did all the fighting in our corps and fought well.

George C. Chandler,
Union soldier from New Jersey, November 5, 1864

When there is no officer with us, we take no prisoners.

Union soldier from Wisconsin, explaining that Union soldiers
were taking revenge for the massacre at Fort Pillow, 1864

The rebels who were captured by the colored troops, gave up with a very bad grace.

> Private Smith, Union soldier from Illinois,
> on watching black troops charge the Confederate lines
> at the battle of Nashville

We have done with hoeing cotton,
we have done with hoeing corn,
We are colored Yankee soldiers,
now, as sure as you are born;
When the masters hear us yelling,
they'll think it's Gabriel's horn,
As we go marching on . . .

> "Marching Song of the First Arkansas (Negro) Regiment,"
> sung to the tune of "Battle Hymn of the Republic"

Words would fail to describe the scene which those who witnessed it will never forget—the welcome given to a regiment of colored troops by their people redeemed from slavery. As shouts, prayers, and blessings resounded on every side, all felt that the hardships and dangers of the siege were fully repaid . . . On through the streets of the rebel city passed the column, on through the chief seat of that slave power, tottering to its fall . . . The glory and the triumph of this hour may be imagined, but can never be described. It was one of those occasions which happen but once in a lifetime, to be lived over in memory for ever.

> Colonel Charles B. Fox of the (African American)
> 54th Massachusetts Volunteers, on the march
> into Charleston, February 17, 1865

The change seems almost miraculous. The very people who, three years ago, crouched at their masters' feet, on the accursed soil of Virginia, now march in a victorious column of freedmen, over the same land.

> Black sergeant, on the march into Richmond, April 1865

African Americans Fighting for the South

We wish to our hearts that the Yankees would whip, and we would have run over to their side but our officers would have shot us if we had made the attempt.

John Parker,
slave pressed into fighting for the Confederacy
at Bull Run, quoted in *Douglass' Monthly*, March 1862

They advanced against us. They mutilated our dead and stripped them naked. They bayoneted our wounded and cut their throats in cold blood . . . It is wrong to bring negroes into battlefields.

Francis Boland, Union soldier,
of Confederate black troops, June 14, 1862

Nobody knows anything about these men who has not seen them in battle.

Colonel Thomas Wentworth Higginson,
1st South Carolina Volunteers,
an African American regiment, January 1863

It would have been madness to attempt, with the bravest white troops, what I have successfully accomplished with black ones.

Colonel Thomas Wentworth Higginson,
1st South Carolina Volunteers,
an African American regiment, January 1863

I never more wish to hear the expression, "the niggers won't fight." Come with me 100 yards from where I sit, and I can show you the wounds that cover the bodies of 16 as brave, loyal and patriotic soldiers as ever drew bead on a Rebel.

Captain M. M. Miller, 9th Regiment,
of Louisiana Volunteers of African Descent,
letter to his aunt, June 10, 1863

Parade stance

Managing the War

Lincoln on the Union Rank and File

He who does something at the head of one Regiment, will eclipse him who does nothing at the head of a hundred.

Abraham Lincoln, letter to Major General David Hunter,
who complained of being banished to Kansas with only
3,000 troops, December 31, 1861

I fully appreciate Gen. Pope's splendid achievements with their invaluable results; but you must know that Major Generalships in the Regular Army, are not as plenty as blackberries.

Abraham Lincoln, letter to Illinois governor Richard Yates
and treasurer William Butler, on their request for
Pope's transfer to the regular army, April 10, 1862

The army is constantly depleted by company officers who give their men leave of absence in the very face of the enemy, and on the very eve of an engagement, which is almost as bad as desertion. At this very moment there are between seventy and one hundred thousand men absent on furlough from the Army of the Potomac. The army, like the nation, has become demoralized by the idea that the war is to be ended, the nation united, and peace restored, by strategy, and not by hard desperate fighting. Why, then, should not the soldiers have furloughs.

Abraham Lincoln, memorandum on furloughs,
November 1862

The courage with which you, in an open field, maintained the contest against an entrenched foe, and the consummate skill and success with which you crossed and re-crossed the river, in face of the enemy, show that you possess all the qualities of a great army, which will yet give victory to the cause of the country and of popular government.

Abraham Lincoln, message to the Union army,
on losing the Battle of Fredericksburg, December 22, 1862

I can make more brigadier generals, but I can't make more horses.

Abraham Lincoln, after Confederate major John Mosby
raided General Edwin Stoughton's headquarters
and took him, 32 other Union officers, and 58 horses,
March 9, 1863

The case of Andrews is really a very bad one, as appears by the record already before me. Yet before receiving this I had ordered his punishment commuted . . . I did this, not on any merit in the case, but because I am trying to evade the butchering business lately.

Abraham Lincoln,
endorsement concerning Henry Andrews,
January 7, 1864

Philosophy of War

Our people are opposed to work. Our troops, officers, Community, and press All ridicule it. It is the very means by which McClellan has & is advancing. Why should we leave to him the whole advantage of labor? Combined with valour, fortitude & boldness, of which we have our fair proportion, it should lead us to success. What carried the Roman soldiers into all Countries but that happy Combination? The evidences of their labor last to this day. There is nothing so military as labour.

Robert E. Lee, Confederate general,
letter to Jefferson Davis, June 1862

Although I had many relatives and hosts of friends serving under the Confederate flag all the time, I never fully realized the fratricidal character of the conflict until I lost my idolized brother Dave of the Southern army one day, and was nursing my Northern husband back to life the next.

Septima Collis, born in Charleston
and wife of a Union officer

The more blood there is shed at the start, the less there will be in the end. The more terrible and decisive the battles, the shorter the campaign.

Richmond Enquirer, 1862

You cannot conduct warfare against savages unless you become half savage yourself.

John Sherman, U.S. senator from Ohio, July 9, 1862

From the summer of 1862, the war became a war of wholesale devastation. From the spring of 1864, it seemed to have become nearly a war of extermination.

John Esten Cooke, Confederate veteran and historian

Men may wrangle and dispute about the causes, but as to these measures, posterity can have but one verdict to pronounce—a verdict of horror and execration.

The *London Times*, of Northern war maneuvers,
quoted in *Camp and Field* by
Reverend Joseph Cross,
Confederate army chaplain, 1864

We are not only fighting hostile armies, but a hostile people, and must make old and young, rich and poor, feel the hand of war.

William T. Sherman, Union general,
Memoirs, 1875

The necessities of state require that all the inhabitants of a hostile country should be treated as enemies whether in arms or not. Even women and children are enemies . . . The humanity of modern civilization does not justify putting them to death unless absolutely necessary.

Thaddeus Stevens, congressman,
Pennsylvania

If a man will win battles and give his brigade a right to brag loudly of its doings, he may have its admiration and even its enthusiastic devotion though he be as pitiless and wicked as Lucifer.

J. W. DeForest, "The Brigade Commander"

I think that, as life is action and passion, it is required of a man that he should share the passion and action of his time at peril of being judged not to have lived.

Oliver Wendell Holmes Jr.,
Memorial Day 1884

Strategy

The keys of the so-called Confederate states are Richmond and New Orleans. When we have taken these our task will be done.

Harper's Weekly, April 1861

No one could say at any hour that he would be living the next. Men were killed in their camps, at their meals, and . . . in their sleep. So many men were daily struck in the camp and trenches that men became utterly reckless, passing about where balls were striking as though it was their normal life.

William Hamilton, Union general under Sherman,
on trench warfare, December 24, 1862

We must make this campaign an active one. Only thus can a weaker country cope with a stronger. It must make up in activity what it lacks in strength.

Stonewall Jackson, Confederate general, 1863

I would not take any risk of being entangled upon the river, like an ox jumped half over a fence, and liable to be torn by dogs, front and rear, without a fair chance to gore one way or kick the other.

Abraham Lincoln,
letter to General Joseph Hooker,
on how to handle Confederate general Robert E. Lee
at the Rappahannock, June 5, 1863

I am heartily tired of hearing what Lee is going to do. Some of you always seem to think he is suddenly going to turn a double somersault, and land on our rear and on both our flanks at the same time. Go back to your command, and try to think what we are going to do ourselves, instead of what Lee is going to do."

Ulysses S. Grant, Union general

General Pickett rode to confer with Alexander, then to the ground upon which I was resting, where he was soon handed a slip of paper. After reading it he handed it to me. It read: *If you are coming at all, come at once, or I cannot give you proper support, but the enemy's fire has not slackened at all. At least eighteen guns are still firing from the cemetary itself. Alexander.*
   Pickett said, "General, shall I advance?"

James Longstreet, Confederate general,
"The Battle of Gettysburg"

Up, men, and to your posts! Don't forget today that you are from Old Virginia!

George Edward Pickett, Confederate general,
command that began Pickett's Charge at Gettysburg, July 3, 1863

It ain't so hard to get to that ridge—the hell of it is to stay there.

Confederate soldier, Pickett's Charge at Gettysburg

When you turned Northward East of the Big Black, I feared it was a mistake. I now wish to make the personal acknowledgment that you were right, and I was wrong.

Abraham Lincoln, letter to General Ulysses S. Grant,
on the Vicksburg Campaign, July 13, 1863

If the Vicksburg campaign meant anything, in a military point of view, it was that there are no fixed laws of war which are not subject to the conditions of the country, the climate, and the habits of the people.

Ulysses S. Grant, Union general

This is a dreadful reminiscence of McClellan. The same spirit moved McC. to claim a victory because Pa. & Md. were safe. The heart of 10 million people sunk within them when McClellan raised that shout last fall. Will our Generals never get that idea out of their heads? The whole country is our soil.

> Abraham Lincoln, on General Meade's order,
> in which he called on his troops to drive
> the invader from "our soil," quoted in White House
> secretary John Hay's diary, July 14, 1863

Three years ago by a little reflection and patience they could have had a hundred years of peace and prosperity . . . Last year they could have saved their slaves, but now it is too late . . . Next year their lands will be taken . . . and in another year they may beg in vain for their lives.

> William T. Sherman, Union general,
> of Southerners, January 1864

Not satisfied with all the destruction which modern science has enabled mankind to wreak upon each other, the North has called to its aid the mighty agencies of nature . . . in cutting the levees, or dams, which keep the Mississippi in its course.

> The *London Times*, quoted in *Camp and Field*
> by Reverend Joseph Cross, Confederate army chaplain, 1864

By the time we reached Cold Harbor we had begun to understand what our new adversary meant, and therefore, for the first time, I think, the men in the ranks of the Army of Northern Virginia realized that the era of experimental campaigns against us was over; that Grant was not going to retreat.

> George Cary Eggleston, Confederate sergeant from Virginia,
> recalling his army's arrival at Cold Harbor, June 1, 1864

They began the war with a contempt for the spade, but now thoroughly believe in it. They use bayonets, tin pans, and even, I am told, split their tin canteens to get a utensil that will throw up earth.

> Josiah Gorgas, chief of ordnance of the Confederate army,
> on the soldiers' respect for entrenchment, June 4, 1864

I propose to fight it out on this line, if it takes all summer.

> Ulysses S. Grant, Union general,
> dispatch to Washington from the field, May 11, 1864

I have seen your dispatch expressing your unwillingness to break your hold where you are. Neither am I willing. Hold on with a bull-dog grip, and chew and choke, as much as possible.

> Abraham Lincoln,
> letter to General Ulysses S. Grant, August 17, 1864

Gen. Sheridan says "If the thing is pressed I think that Lee will surrender." Let the thing be pressed.

> Abraham Lincoln,
> letter to General Ulysses S. Grant, April 7, 1865

It has happened as I told them in Richmond it would happen. The line has been stretched until it is broken.

> Robert E. Lee, Confederate general, on the crumbling of
> the Confederate lines in the Spring of 1865

Get there first with the most.

> Nathan Bedford Forrest, Confederate general,
> on how to win a war

Plunder

No Goths or vandals ever had less respect for the lives & property or friends and foes, and henceforth, we ought never to hope for any friends in Virginia.

> William T. Sherman, Union general,
> on his troops' tendency to steal and burn,
> incurring the hostility of the populace, Summer 1861

The country seems possessed by demons, black and white.

> Kate Stone, Louisiana,
> on the plunder around her plantation

I, poor innocent, would not let a soldier take a green apple or a fence rail.

> William T. Sherman, Union general, of his behavior
> in Kentucky in 1861, when secessionists burned the homes
> of Unionists, but Sherman restrained the Union army

Men of the South! shall our mothers, our wives, our daughters and our sisters, be thus outraged by the ruffianly soldiers of the North, to whom it is given the right to treat, at their pleasure, the ladies of the South as common harlots? Arouse friends, and drive back from our soil, those infamous invaders of our homes and disturbers of our family ties.

> Pierre Beauregard, Confederate general,
> General Orders No. 44, May 19, 1862

I asked one man how he would like for his mother and sisters to be so treated, he said if they were rebels he would think it all right.

> Margaret Crozier Ramsey, Knoxville,
> of Union soldiers who pillaged her home

We are here and can see where the excuse is for many things that you call abuses.

> Union soldier from Wisconsin,
> letter to his father, Summer 1863

I resolved to leave no ruins along the line of my march through Pennsylvania; no marks of a more enduring character than the tracks of my soldiers along its superb pikes.

> John B. Gordon, Confederate general,
> to the Army of Northern Virginia, June 1863

Like bees going to a Hive, the Boys one after another would crowd on to the Porch, into the Hall. Parlor, Kitchen or Bedroom, appropriating every thing useful or ornamental which they thought they could take care of.

Joseph Lester, Union soldier, on plunder, August 23, 1863

No spite seemed too small for them to indulge in. They stole for the mere pleasure of stealing, for they made no use, nor could they of much they stole and destroyed.

Grace Elmore, South Carolina,
on the Union soldiers who plundered her home

[O]ur familys have no protection the white soldiers break into our houses act as they please steal our chickens rob our gardens and if any one defends their-Selves against them they are taken to the gard house for it.

Richard Etheredge and William Benson,
soldiers of the 36th U.S. Colored Regiment,
in a letter to Union general Oliver O. Howard

I have seen women crying & begging for them to leave a little for the children, but their tears were of no avail . . . Some of our soldiers are a disgrace to the service.

David Nichol, Union soldier, May 21, 1864

A crow flying over the valley would have to carry his own provisions.

Popular comment on the ravaging of the Shenandoah Valley
by Union generals Hunter and Sheridan, Winter 1864

I must tell you how shamefully Gen. Wheeler's men acted. Though they have a wide-spread reputation of being the greatest horse thieves in the country, they never acted worse than they have recently. While the enemy were burning and

destroying property, on one side of Briar creek, they were stealing horses and
mules on the other.

> Confederate woman, of Union soldiers,
> letter to the *Countryman*, January 1865

I have travelled a heap of late, and had occasion to retire into some very
sequestered regions, but nary hill or holler, nary mountain gorge or inaccessi-
ble ravine have I found, but what the cavalry had been there, and just left.
And that is the reason they can't be whipped, for they have always just left,
and took an odd horse or two with 'em.

> Bill Arp, Confederate humorist, on the Confederate cavalry,
> notorious for plundering the Southern countryside

Homefront—The North

A group of respectable New Yorkers tried to get their countrymen to write a
national hymn that summer, and when the entries were submitted, found
themselves the nation's largest collectors of waste-paper. Four or five bales of
made-to-order songs arrived in one afternoon; most of them could be
described as the first wartime atrocities.

> Mark Wahlgren Summers, historian, on the Summer of 1861

I am more a wife than a patriot, & although I do care for my country, I care for
you much more.

> Ann Cotton, Marietta, Ohio,
> letter to her husband, a Union surgeon, January 1, 1863

A perfect reign of terror exists in the quarters of this helpless people, and if
the troubles which now agitate our city, continue during the week it is
believed that not a single negro will remain within the metropolitan limits.

> *New York Herald*, reporting on the draft/race riots
> in New York City, July 15, 1863

This young man who was murdered by the mob on the corner of Twenty-seventh St., and Seventh Avenue, was a quiet, inoffensive man, 23 years of age . . . A short time previous to the assault upon his person, he called upon his mother to see if anything could be done by him for her safety. The old lady, who is noted for her piety and her Christian deportment, said she considered herself perfectly safe; but if her time to die had come, she was ready to die. Her son then knelt down by her side, and implored the protection of Heaven in behalf of his mother . . . Scarcely had the supplicant risen from his knees, when the mob broke down the door, seized him, beat him over the head and face with fists and clubs, and then hanged him in the presence of his mother.

> *Report of the Committee of Merchants*
> *for the Relief of Colored People,*
> *Suffering from the Late Riots*
> *of the City of New York, 1863*

I was left almost senseless, with a broken arm and a face covered with blood, on the railroad track . . . I entertain no malice and have no desire for revenge against these people. Why should they hurt me or my colored brethren? We are poor men like them; we work hard and get but little for it.

> Statement by an elderly whitewasher,
> *Report of the Committee of Merchants*
> *for the Relief of Colored People, Suffering*
> *from the Late Riots of the City of New York, 1863*

The fact is the people have not made up their minds that we are at war with the South.

> Abraham Lincoln,
> to a delegation of the Sanitary Commission

The people are wild for peace.

> Thurlow Weed, New York Republican,
> on why Abraham Lincoln could not be reelected in 1864

Homefront—The South

A dog fight, a scared horse, a smoking chimney, or a runaway negro, is all that is necessary to put the people in a stir.

> Alabaman reporter, of the excitement that reigned
> in Montgomery during the Confederate Convention,
> February 1861

War, war! is the one idea. The children play only with toy cannons and soldiers; the oldest inhabitant goes by every day with his rifle to practice; the public squares are full of companies drilling, and are now the fashionable resorts.

> G., a pro-Union woman from New Orleans,
> diary entry, April 20, 1861

As for reading I have long given that up. I do not remember when I turn a page what was on the other side.

> Catherine Ann Edmonston, North Carolina,
> diary entry, May 18, 1861

There is no people in the world so crazy with military madness.

> William H. Russell, correspondent to
> the London Times, on the citizens
> and troops of Alabama, May 7, 1861

I thought you would not speak to me. I thought all you wanted to do was to fill up the roads with logs and brush so that Lincoln's Army could not pass through the country.

> Pellona Alexander, letter to her husband,
> a Confederate soldier, describing a dream
> in which he had gone mad and had to be
> brought home, April 14, 1862

To be rich during the War was considered a disgrace. Almost every person of note was suffering from poverty, and people were proud of it. Every one gave freely to the cause.

Annie Laurie Broidrick, Southerner

I say it is time to proclaim to every Winchester in the so-called Southern confederacy that there shall not be left one article above ground in such a town that fire can consume.

L. E. Chittendon, when Confederate troops
entered Maryland, September 1862, alluding to
Northern restraint in not burning Winchester, Virginia

I went in to tell Ma & Pa. How I did hate to do it. Poor Pa & Ma. Pa got up. He has been walking the floor all day. He says his peace is broken forever on this earth. His only boy, his pride, the idol of Ma's heart.

Rachel Craighead, Nashville, on informing her parents
of the death of her brother, Bud, October 20, 1862

I send my willing contribution of flowers as an offering to the gallant dead of the Richmond Light Infantry Blues, of which my husband was once a musician, and who fell in the service. I hope they all sleep sweetly "across the river under the shade of the trees" to rise again at another trumpet, as lovely and fresh as these flowers, to flourish forever in the mansions of the blest.

Judith C. Judah, in memory of "A Colored Southern Soldier"

No cripples from the battle-fields are these—they can sing and dance; they can mimic fighting on the stage. For the serious work of repelling the enemy they have neither taste nor heart. But they can sing while the country groans, and dance while the carts are bringing, in sad funeral procession, the dead to their very doors.

John Lansing Burrows, Baptist minister,
sermon decrying the opening of a theater
in Richmond, February 8, 1863

Since I first heard that my darling had been killed I have through every discouragement from friends & circumstances, entertained the hope that he was living, that I shall yet welcome him to his home.

> Mary Martha Reid, matron-nurse, Richmond,
> on her son, February 26, 1863

A pair of old coat sleeves saved—nothing is thrown away now—was in my trunk. I cut an exact pattern from my old shoes, laid it on the sleeves, and cut out thus good uppers and sewed them carefully; then soaked the soles and sewed the cloth to them. I am so proud of these home-made shoes, think I'll put them in a glass case when the war is over, as an heirloom.

> G., a pro-Union woman from New Orleans,
> diary entry, April 28, 1863

One woman demanded to see my authority to search her house . . . I pointed her to a line of soldiers standing in front of the house and told her there was my authority and the power to enforce it.

> John A. Clark, Union officer, August 10, 1863

Soldiers know how to respect soldiers—citizens do not.

> G. W. Logan,
> Confederate soldier from Kentucky, August 12, 1863

All classes, all trades, all profession, and both sexes alas! seemed infected by the foul contagion.

> William W. Bennett, on extortion and
> profiteering in the South

I want all blankets and carpets that can possibly be spared. I want them, ladies of Alabama, to shield your noble defenders against an enemy more to be dreaded than the Northern foe with musket in hand—the snows of coming winter . . . Every one, male or female, who can furnish a blanket may save a man to the army.

W. M. Gillespie, Confederate captain,
newspaper appeal to the ladies of Alabama, October 1863

Aunty had been ordered to leave her beautiful home to give place to a Yankee colonel who had given her only half a day to move all her property. O cruel soldier! could you not be a little more lenient? Could you not allow her one day for this work?

Mary Rawson, during the occupation of Atlanta, 1864

Immediately is a quick word, gentlemen, to a man who has lived at a place 40 years.

Warner Underwood, Unionist of Kentucky,
on receiving word from the Confederate army
that he must abandon his house immediately

The cotton floated down the Mississippi one sheet of living flame, even in the sunlight. It would have been grand at night.

Sarah Morgan, Baton Rouge,
on the planters' burning of their cotton to
prevent the Union army from seizing it

Whether 'tis nobler in the Confederacy to suffer the pangs of unappeasable hunger and never-ending troubles, or to take passage to a Yankee port, and there remaining, end them.

Sarah Morgan, Baton Rouge, on deciding whether
to try to flee the Union army, or seek the protection
of her Union-sympathizing brother in New Orleans

"Colonel Cooke," I asked humbly enough, for I was ready then to take infor-
mation and advice from anybody, "how long do you think it will be before the
army comes back?"
"Can't say, madam."
"Would you advise me to wait here until its return?"
"Can't say, madam."
"Would you advise me to go to Richmond?"
"Madam, I would advise you to go to Richmond."
"You think then it will be some time before the army returns?"
"I can't say, madam."
I felt like shaking him and asking: "What *can* you say?"

> Myrta Lockett Avery, whose husband served
> under Confederate general Jeb Stuart,
> *A Virginia Girl in the Civil Wary 1861-1865*

Echoes

The supreme tactical fact of the war was that the rifle had made defense
three times as strong as offense.

> J.F.C. Fuller, major general of the British Army, 1933

Lincoln was a realist and Davis was not.

> Robert Penn Warren, *The Legacy of the Civil War*,
> comparing the two men's approaches to civil liberties

Grant's Wilderness campaign had cost him more than 50,000 casualties.
During the campaign's progress, Washington sent him about 40,000 reinforcements. President Lincoln accepted the horrendous casualty reports without
protest, but he must have agonized over them in private. They affected him
not only as a man of conscience but as a politician. This was the Presidential
election year, and his conduct of the war was the leading issue.

> Richard Wheeler, *Voices of the Civil War*, 1976

Wounded Zouave in deserted camp

Foreign Opinion and Involvement

There they are cutting each other's throats, because one half of them prefer hiring their servants for life, and the other by the hour.

Thomas Carlyle, 19th-century British historian

They will never recognize our independence until our conquering sword hangs dripping over the prostrate heads of the North.

William Yancey, ardent secessionist from Alabama,
of European recognition of the Confederacy, 1861

A more ridiculous sight than a lot of native-born Americans, not understanding a word of French, beating their breasts as they howled what they flattered themselves were the words of the song, it was never my bad fortune to witness.

> James M. Morgan, *Recollections of a Rebel Reefer*,
> on Confederate revelers attempting to sing the "Marseillaise"

The dread of war with the United States is a national bugbear.

> Henry Hotze, Confederate propaganda agent
> in England, letter to the Confederate secretaries
> of state, February 28, 1862

There is a land—part of this your own continent—which we wish to go. It is that portion generally called Central America. There are lands there without inhabitants, yet bearing spontaneously all that is suited to our race.

> Petition to Congress signed by 40
> African Americans asking for Congress to sponsor
> their resettlement in Central America, April 1862

Take away *time is money*, and what is left of England? Take away *cotton is king*, and what is left of America?

> Victor Hugo, *Les Miserables*, 1862

England has been jealous of the United States to an inordinate degree. She has clearly foreseen that, if they continue united, they must become, before the close of this century, the first nation of the world . . . Thus, in addition to the old grudge, she has been stimulated by the fear of losing her position among the powers of the earth. Cost what it might, she has felt that for her the greatest of all objects has been to destroy the Union. She has succeeded at last, and it is not wonderful that she should desire to see the war carried on as long as both parties may have the strength to maintain themselves. She feels that intervention would follow recognition, and this she is by no means disposed to undertake, because it might have the effect of shortening the war.

> *Southern Illustrated News*, on "Why We Have Not
> Yet Been Acknowledged by Great Britain," October 4, 1862

They say that recognition
Will the Rebel country save,
But Johnny Bull and Mister France
Are 'fraid of Uncle Abe.

> "We'll Fight for Uncle Abe," Union fighting song

Jefferson Davis and other leaders of the South have made an army; they are
making, it appears, a navy; and they have made what is more than either—
they have made a nation.

> W. E. Gladstone, chancellor of the exchequer
> of Great Britain, October 7, 1862

The privileged classes all over Europe rejoice in the thoughts of the ruin of
the great experiment in popular government.

> Charles Francis Adams, U.S. minister
> to the Court of St. James, December 25, 1862

America, teacher of liberty to our Fathers, now opens the most solemn Era of
human progress, and whilst she amazes the world by her gigantic boldness,
makes us sadly reflect that this old Europe albeit agitated by the grand cause of
human freedom, does not understand, nor move forward to become equal to her.

> G., M., and N. Garibaldi, Italian nationalists,
> letter to Abraham Lincoln regarding emancipation,
> August 6, 1863

The Emancipation Proclamation has done more for us here than all our former victories and all our diplomacy.

> Henry Adams, secretary to the U.S. minister to
> the Court of St. James, letter to his brother, 1863

Not that a human being cannot justly own another but that he cannot own
him unless he is loyal to the United States.

> London *Spectator*, on the principle behind the
> Emancipation Proclamation, which applied only
> to the Confederate states

It would be superfluous in me to point out to your Lordship that this is war.

> Charles Francis Adams, U.S. minister to the
> Court of St. James, warning the British foreign
> secretary not to let European-made ironclad warships
> through to the Confederacy, September 5, 1863

[I wonder] whether any of us will be able to live contented in times of peace and laziness. Our generation has been stirred up from its lowest layers and there is that in its history which will stamp every member of it until we are all in our graves. We cannot be commonplace . . . One does every day and without a second thought, what at another time would be the event of a year, perhaps of a life.

> Henry Adams, secretary to the U.S. minister
> to the Court of St. James

There is certainly not one government in Europe but is watching the war in this country with the ardent prayer that the United States may be effectually split, crippled, and dismembered by it. There is not one but would help toward that dismemberment, if it dared.

> Walt Whitman, 1864

Because it has the largest purse.

> Baron Rothschild, London banker,
> when asked why he predicted the North would win the war

It has been now about four years since I heard from you and I must say I am over anxious to hear from you once more. More so since I heard the war is over.

> William Douglass, one of hundreds of African Americans
> sent to Liberia during the colonization movement

Gettysburg dead

War, Duty, and Honor

Let us have faith that right makes might, and in that faith, let us, to the end, dare to do our duty as we understand it.

Abraham Lincoln,
address to the Cooper Institute, February 27, 1860

Duty is the sublimest word in our language. Do your duty in all things. You cannot do more. You should never wish to do less.

Robert E. Lee, Confederate general

My duty is to obey orders.

Stonewall Jackson, Confederate general

The Colored man is like A lost sheep Meney of them old and young was Brave and Active. But has Bin hurrided By and ignominious Death into Eternity. But I hope God will Presearve the Rest Now in existance to Get Justice and Rights we have to Do our Duty or Die and no help for us It is true the country is in A hard struggle But we All must Remember Mercy and Justice Grate and small. it is Devine.

African American soldier

Great men, great nations, have not been boasters and buffoons, but perceivers of the terror of life, and have manned themselves to face it.

Ralph Waldo Emerson, "Fate," *The Conduct of Life*, 1860

I never before wished I was a man—now I feel so keenly my weakness and dependence. I cannot do or say anything—for "it would be unbecoming in a young lady." How I should love to fight and even die for my Country—our glorious beautiful South—what a privilege I should esteem it, but am denied it because I am a woman.

Alice Ready, Southerner

War is altogether stupid as well as horrible.

Mary Johnston, post war novelist, Virginia

I used to think war was a science, but its a mistake . . . the great majority of battles are the result of axident. And the results are the results of axidents.

Thomas Edwin Smith, Union officer

War is far less evil than degradation.

New York Times, April 16, 1861

Wars are not all evil, they are part of the grand machinery by which this world is governed.

William T. Sherman, Union general

When Duty and Honor call him, it would be strange if I were to influence him to remain "in the lap of inglorious ease" when so much is at stake.

Ella Gertrude Clanton Thomas,
North Carolina, July 13, 1861

I could not wish you away from the place of danger, for duty and honor demand that every true man should "take his life in his hand" & stand ready to defend his family & his country.

Julia Fisher, Florida, letter to her husband, November 1861

Johnnie, if a boy dies for his country the glory is his forever, isn't it?

Wounded Confederate soldier from Kentucky to John Green,
at the Battle of Shiloh, April 6–7, 1862

Our men are not sufficiently impressed with a sense of honor that it is better to die by fire than to run.

William Hardee, Confederate general, April 9, 1862

The dogmas of the quiet past, are inadequate to the stormy present.

Abraham Lincoln,
annual message to Congress, December 1, 1862

But what a cruel thing is war, to separate and destroy families and friends, and mar the purest joys and happiness God has granted us in this world; to fill our hearts with hatred instead of love for our neighbors, and to devastate the fair face of this beautiful world.

> Robert E. Lee, Confederate general,
> letter to his wife, Christmas 1862

Mother whose heart hung humble as a button
On the bright splendid shroud of your son,
Do not weep.
War is kind.

> Stephen Crane, "War is Kind"

It is well that war is so terrible, or we should grow too fond of it.

> Robert E. Lee, Confederate general,
> on the Union retreat at Fredericksburg, December 1862

He is the soldier citizen: he could face the flame of battle for his country: he can also earn his own living. He could leave his office-chair to march and fight for three years; and he can return to peaceful industry, as ennobling as his fighting.

It is in millions of such men that the strength of the Republic consists.

> J. W. DeForest,
> *Miss Ravenel's Conversion from Secession to Loyalty*

War is a strange scale for measuring men.

> Harry Lewish, Confederate soldier, August 20, 1863

And now, he is in the War: and how has he conducted himself? Let their dusky forms rise up, out the mires of James Island, and give the answer. Let the rich mould around Wagners parapets be upturned, and there will be found an Eloquent answer. Obedient and patient, and Solid as wall are they. all we lack, is a paler hue, and a better acquaintance with the Alphabet.

> James Henry Gooding, African American soldier,
> in response to his own rhetorical question, "Had
> black men done their duty as soldiers?" September 28, 1863

This war has entirely changed the American character . . . Ideas of cheapness and economy are thrown to the winds. The individual who makes the most money—no matter how—and spends the most money—no matter for what— is considered the greatest man. To be extravagant is to be fashionable . . . The world has seen its iron age, its silver age, its golden age and its brazen age. This is the age of the shoddy.

> *New York Herald*, October 6, 1863

On principle I dislike an oath which requires a man to swear he has not done wrong. It rejects the Christian principle of forgiveness on terms of repentance. I think it is enough if the man does no wrong hereafter.

> Abraham Lincoln, to Edwin M. Stanton, U.S. secretary of war,
> on the Oath of Allegiance, February 5, 1864

How about that oath of allegiance? is what I frequently ask myself, and always an uneasy qualm of conscience troubles me. Guilty or not guilty of perjury? According to the law of God in the abstract, and of nations, Yes; according to my conscience, Jeff Davis, and the peculiar position I was placed in, No.

> Sarah Morgan, Baton Rouge, on the Oath of Allegiance
> demanded of citizens by occupying Union forces

They say to us, "This Oath or see yourselves plundered by Yankees and negroes alike; This Oath or turned out of your house and loved home." Swear anything—both possible and impossible—say light is darkness—heat is cold— . . . Yankees are honest—what you will! I assent to it all, and hate you while I do it.

> Catherine Devereux Edmondston, Southerner

I had rather our throats were all cut, or turned beggars on the world than that Bro. John should disgrace himself by taking that dirty oath.

Kate Carney, Murfreesboro, Tennessee

The oath was as strong as the English language could make it: to uphold the government of the United States in act and in words, almost in our very thoughts; to pledge eternal enmity to the rebellion and all engaged in it; to give them no assistance, nor hold any communication with them directly or indirectly. Finally we swore that we took this oath freely and voluntarily and below, where the name was signed was printed, "The penalty for the violation of this oath is death."

Lizzie Hardin, Harrodsburg, Kentucky,
on the Oath of Allegiance

War is a dredful thing, but their never was such A war as this & I sincearly hope their never will be Again.

W. A. James, Confederate soldier, June 1864

There is glory for the brave
Who lead, and nobly save,
But no knowledge in the grave
Where the nameless followers sleep.

Herman Melville (1819–1891),
"Sheridan at Cedar Creek," October 1864

The glory of History is indifferent to events: it is simply Honour.

Edward A. Pollard, Confederate editor,
"A Letter on the State of the War," 1865

People who have never been through a war don't know anything about war. May I never pass through another. Why will men fight? Especially brothers?

Why cannot they adjust their differences and redress their wrongs without the shedding of woman's tears and the spilling of each other's blood.

Malvina Black Gist, Confederate war widow, 1865

Who is to blame for all this waste of human life? . . . And what does it amount to? Has there been anything gained by all this sacrifice? What were we fighting for, the principles of slavery?

Samuel T. Foster, Confederate captain, April 1865

The rights and interests of the colored citizens of Virginia are more directly, immediately and deeply affected in the restoration of the State to the Federal Union than any other class of citizens . . . we have peculiar claims to be heard in regard to the question of reconstruction, and . . . we cannot keep silent without dereliction of duty to ourselves, to our country, and to our God.

African American meeting at Bute Street Baptist
Church, Norfolk, Virginia, a month after war's end

It is a severe but just commentary on the dominion of passion and prejudice over reason, that great and revolutionary changes in political organization are rarely made except by bloodshed.

Durbin Ward, Union general,
at a Federal veterans' reunion, 1868

There is nothing intellectual about fighting. It is the fit work of brutes and brutish men. And in modern war, where men are organized in masses and converted into insensate machines, there is really nothing heroic or romantic or in any way calculated to appeal to the imagination.

John Esten Cooke, Confederate veteran and historian,
in conversation years afterward

There is something exhilarating in the bravery which will dare a great danger.

Mary Tucker Magill, *Chronicles of the Late War*, 1871

War is at best barbarism . . . Its glory is all moonshine. It is only those who have neither fired a shot, nor heard the shrieks and groans of the wounded who cry aloud for blood, more vengeance, more desolation. War is hell.

> William T. Sherman, Union general,
> address at the Michigan Military Academy, June 19, 1879

In the midst of doubt, in the collapse of creeds, there is one thing I do not doubt, and that is that the faith is true and adorable which leads a soldier to throw away his life in obedience to a blindly accepted duty, in a cause which he little understands, in a plan of campaign of which he has no notion, under tactics of which he does not see the use.

> Oliver Wendell Holmes Jr., former Union officer,
> Memorial Day address entitled "The Soldier's Faith," 1895

I could have taken no other course without dishonor & if all was to be done over again I should act precisely in the same manner.

> Robert E. Lee, Confederate general,
> after the war, on fighting for the Confederacy

Echoes

Everybody knows which side has won before there is a war, everybody knows it, but nobody likes to believe it, and then they make a war.

> Gertrude Stein, *Four in America*

We are celebrating Antietam, where if a bullet had gone one eighth of an inch differently the chances are that I should not be writing to you.

> Oliver Wendell Holmes Jr., in *The Soldier's Faith,*
> demonstrating his oft-expressed pride in the fact
> that he survived the Battle of Antietam, 1927

Sunday morning mass at Camp Cass, 9th Massachusetts Infantry, USA, 1861

God and Religion

One with God is always a majority.

Wendell Phillips, abolitionist

Oh, thou heart-searching God, we trust that thou sees we are pursuing those rights which were guaranteed to us by the solemn covenants of our fathers, and which were cemented by their blood.

Reverend Basil Manly,
prayer to open the Confederate Convention, February 4, 1861

Mine eyes have seen the glory of the coming of the Lord:
He is trampling out the vintage where the grapes of wrath are stored;
He hath loosed the fateful lightning of his terrible swift sword:
His truth is marching on.

I have seen Him in the watch fires of a hundred circling camps;
They have builded him an altar in the evening dew and damps;
I can read His righteous sentence by the dim and flaring lamps.
His day is marching on.

I have read a fiery gospel writ in burnished rows of steel:
"As you deal with my contemners, so with you my grace shall deal;
Let the Hero, born of woman, crush the serpent with his heel,
Since God is marching on."

Julia Ward Howe, from "Battle Hymn of the Republic"

Young man I think I know you—I think this face is the face of the Christ himself,
Dead and divine and brother of all, and here again he lies.

Walt Whitman (1819-1892),
"A Sight in Camp in the Daybreak Gray and Dim"

O God I pray the[e] to Direct a bullet or a bayonet to pirce the Hart or
every northern soldier that invade southern Soile . . . I all so ask the[e] to aide
the Southern Confedercy in maintaining Ower rites & establishing the confederate Government.

Plantation overseer, south of New Orleans, June 13, 1861

My mistress was a dreadful pious woman. She would pray ever so long in the
morning, then come out and sit down in her rocking chair, with her cowhide
[whip] and cut and slash everybody who passed her . . . Sometimes I was
afraid she was not a Christian, but she was mighty pious.

Virginia slave

Why should Christians be at all disturbed about the dissolution of the
Union? It can only come by God's permission, and will only be permitted, if
for his people's good.

Stonewall Jackson, Confederate general

The God of humanity is not the God of slavery. If so, shame upon such a God.
I scorn him. If the Bible sanctions slavery, the Bible is a self-evident falsehood.

Henry Wright, abolitionist minister from Massachusetts

Which of these two Christian people are [we] to pray for?

British citizen,
on the moral dilemma of a nation fighting itself

I'm on the Lord's side.

Slave's response to the question of which side he favored

Mother! when around your child
You clasp your arms in love,
And when with grateful joy you raise
Your eyes to God above,
Think of the negro mother, when
Her child is torn away,
Sold for a little slave—oh then,
For that poor mother pray!

Refrain sewn into a quilt sold at anti-slavery fairs

This is God's War, in spite of uncertain generals, in spite of ill success; in spite
of our own unworthiness; the cause is that of the human race, and must prevail.

Hannah Ropes, Georgetown nurse

I think and work with all my power to bring the troops to the right place at the right time; then I have done my duty. As soon as I order them into battle, I leave my army in the hands of God.

Robert E. Lee, Confederate general

Mr. Lincoln would like to have God on his side, but he must have Kentucky.

Abolitionist gibe at Lincoln,
for delaying issue of the Emancipation Proclamation
for fear of losing the Border South

I feel that I would like to shoot a Yankee, and yet I know that this would not be in harmony with the Spirit of Christianity.

Mississippi lawyer, August 1861

I think that the damned old cuss of a Preacher lied like Dixie for he sayed that God has fought our battle and won our victorys. Now if he has done all that why is it not in the papers and why has he not been promoted.

Albinus Fell, sergeant, Union army, April 1862

Surely God has been with mee hee has kept me in the hollow of his hand.

R. F. Eppes, Confederate soldier, July 13, 1862

Never since Adam was planted in the garden of Eden did a holier cause engage the hearts and arms of any nation.

War correspondent to the Savannah *Republican,*
after the second Battle of Bull Run, August 28–30, 1862

The Rebels can afford to give up all their church bells, cow bells and dinner bells to Beauregard, for they never go to church now, their cows have all been taken by foraging parties and they have no dinner to be summoned to.

> Louisville *Courier*, on General Beauregard's
> appeal to Mississippi planters to give over their bells
> to be melted down for cannon, 1862

God ordered otherwise.

> Robert E. Lee, Confederate general,
> on why the Confederates didn't win
> at Chancellorsville, General Orders No. 5, May 7, 1863

God is our only refuge and our strength . . . Let us confess our many sins, and beseech him to give us a higher courage, a purer patriotism and more determined will: that he will convert the hearts of our enemies: that he will hasten the time when war, with its sorrows and sufferings, shall cease, and that he will give us a name and place among the nations of the earth.

> Robert E. Lee, Confederate general, General Orders No. 83,
> directing observance of a day of prayer, August 13, 1863

God is in this war. He will lead us on to victory.

> Jerry Sullivan, ex-slave and soldier,
> at a recruitment meeting in Nashville, November 20, 1863

I want to be able to read the Bible before I die.

> One man's expectations,
> John Tyler's school for African Americans, September 1861

Yours is a holy cause a just cause and may the God of battle watch over and protect you is my constant prayer.

> Lois Davis, Dracut, Massachusetts,
> letter to her sons, February 19, 1864

It seems like the Lord has turned his face from us and left us to work out our own destruction.

J. M. Davis, Confederate soldier under General Johnston,
facing General Sherman across the Chattahoochee River,
July 6, 1864

We hoped for a happy termination of this terrible war long before this; but God knows best, and has ruled otherwise . . . Surely He intends some great good to follow this mighty convulsion, which no mortal could make, and no mortal could stay.

Abraham Lincoln, letter to Eliza Gurney,
wife of a prominent anti-slavery and anti-war
English Quaker, September 4, 1864

Crackers and oats are more necessary to my army than any moral or religious authority.

William T. Sherman, Union general,
denying ministers passes to ride the railroad
to the front, 1864

It is so hard to believe that war is a punishment to a nation, administered by a merciful and just God. If it was a fiery ordeal through which we would come out purified and humbled, I could see the mercy of it; but it seems to me that people are more reckless and sinful than ever. It ruins our young men and has an immoral effect upon everyone. But, of course, it is just and wise, as God orders it so.

Lucy Breckinridge, 1864

Both read the same Bible and pray to the same God; and each invokes His aid against the other. It may seem strange that any men should dare to ask a just God's assistance in wringing their bread from the sweat of other men's faces; but let us not judge that we be not judged.

Abraham Lincoln, second Inaugural Address,
March 4, 1865

Fondly do we hope—fervently do we pray—that this mighty scourge of war may speedily pass away. Yet, if God wills that it continue, until all the wealth piled by the bond-man's two hundred and fifty years of unrequited toil shall be sunk, and until every drop of blood drawn with the lash, shall be paid with another drawn with the sword, as was said three thousand years ago, so still it must be said "the judgments of the Lord, are true and righteous altogether."

Abraham Lincoln, second Inaugural Address,
March 4, 1865

If you kill me I shall go straight to heaven. I am a Christian.

Mary Hort, to a Union officer holding a pistol
to her head, April 1865

Oh, Jesus tell you once before,
    Babylon's fallin' to rise no more;
To go in peace an' sin no more;
    Babylon's fallin' to rise no more.

Song sung by African Americans
at the fall of Richmond, the South's Babylon

Not until the demands of justice had been satisfied; not until we had offered up a bloody holocaust of half a million slain, did God roll back the over-arching cloud of lowering doom.

A. C. Little, Union veteran, 1868

Confederate artillery near Charleston

A Soldier's Life

✰ ✰ ✰

Reflections on a Soldier's Life

A soldier has a hard life and but little consideration.

Robert E. Lee, Confederate general, to his wife

Here we had the first realization of the fact, that we were actual soldiers, and had the first lesson illustrated to us, that a soldier must be patient under wrong, and that he is remediless under injustice—that he, although the self-constituted and acknowledged champion of liberty, has nevertheless, for the time being, parted with that boon.

Nicholas A. Davis, chaplain of Hood's Texas Brigade,
of the brigade's march toward Richmond, Summer 1861

They are good in a dash, but fail in intensity.

William Hardee, Confederate general,
on Confederate soldiers, April 9, 1862

Six months ago a soldier was the greatest thing in the world but now they are worse than the devil not countenanced by nobody at all but the soldiers.

Habun R. Foster, Confederate soldier from Virginia, 1862

Certain military authors who never heard a bullet whistle have written copiously for the marines, to the general effect that fighting is delightful. It is not; it is just tolerable; you can put up with it; but you can't honestly praise it. Bating a few flashes of elation which come in moments of triumph or in the height of a breathless charge, when "the air is all a yell and the earth is all a flame," it is much like being in a rich cholera district in the height of the season.

J. W. DeForest, *A Volunteer's Adventures:*
A Union Captain's Record of the Civil War

A soldier's life is a sucession of extreems, first a long period of inactivity folowed by a time when all his energies both mental and physical are taxed to the utmost.

James T. Miller, Union soldier, May 24, 1863

Yesterday a freeman—today a slave.

Allen Geer, Union volunteer from Illinois,
on joining the army

The interest I once took in the military is almost gone. I do my duty like a machine that has so much in a day to do anyway.

David Bradley, Union officer,
letter to his mother, June 21, 1863

Aimless is military life, except betimes its aim is deadly. Idle life blends with violent death-struggles till the man is unmade a man . . . Of a man he is made a soldier, which is a man-destroying machine.

Cyrus Pringle, Quaker drafted into the Union army,
The Civil War Diary of Cyrus Pringle, August 26, 1863

These are the first "Cartridges" that I have ever seen, and is it possible that we are actually to kill men? Human beings?

Edmund DeWitt Patterson, Confederate soldier,
on being issued ammunition

A man ceases to be himself when he enlists in the ranks.

Leonidas L. Polk, Confederate lieutenant
from North Carolina, 1863

If I could only go off somewhere and have a good cry, put on some clean clothes, get a letter from home . . . I would be ready to come back and die like a Christian.

Paul Vaughn, Union sergeant from Connecticut,
describing what he said to his commanding officer
during the siege of Port Hudson, August 3, 1863

Death is the common lot of all and the diferance between dyeing to day and to morrow is not much but we all prefer to morrow.

M. P. Larry, Union soldier from Maine, February 1864

This is a very demoralizing kind of life. So hardening to human feelings. I can now walk over a battlefield and see the ground strewed with dead bodies, or see a man's limb amputated without any of that tendency of fainting that the sight of blood used to cause.

Richard Webb, Confederate regimental chaplain, May 26, 1864

No negro on Red River but has a happy time compare with that of a Confederate soldier.

Edwin Fay, Confederate soldier from Louisiana

The North Views the South

The rule in North Carolina seems to be that it takes two houses to make a town & that three and a barn constitute a city.

Samuel Storrow, Union soldier from Massachusetts,
November 26, 1862

This Mississippi mud is the nastiest slipperiest stuff you ever saw.

John Crosby, Union sergeant from Connecticut,
January 3, 1863

I thought I'd seen some swamps in trout fishing but these Louisiana swamp took all the conceit out of me.

John Crosby, Union sergeant from Connecticut,
April 5, 1863

Again there was the dreamy delight of ascending an unknown stream, beneath a sinking moon, into a region where peril made fascination. Since the time of the first explorers, I suppose that those Southern waters have known no sensations so dreamy and bewitching as those which this war has brought forth.

Thomas Wentworth Higginson, African American
writer from Boston, excerpt from *Army Life in a Black Regiment*,
in which he describes his trip on an armed steamer
up the St. John's River in Florida

Cottonville is no place at all; if you abolish the name, there is nothing left.

Calvin Aimsworth, Union soldier from Michigan,
April 14, 1864

This place would be quite pleasant if it had been all burned up.

John Crosby, Union soldier from Connecticut,
on Donaldsonville, Louisiana, July 27, 1863

The country about here reminds me more of New England than any place I
have seen and the climate reminds me more of that infernal place down below
that I have not seen but often heard of.

Henry C. Hall, Union sergeant from New England,
on Fredericksburg, August 10, 1862

I danced an American cotillion with Mrs. Manly; it was very violent exercise,
and not the least like any thing I had seen before. A gentleman stands by
shouting out the different figures to be performed, and every one obeys his
orders with much gravity and energy.

Sir Arthur James Lyon Fremantle,
Three Months in the Southern States, 1864

This country is so beautiful I wish I had been born here.

Edward Whitaker, Union corporal from Connecticut,
on northern Virginia, June 24, 1861

In Camp

I see before me now a traveling army halting,
Below a fertile valley spread, with barns and the orchards of summer . . .
The numerous camp-fires scatter'd near and far, some away up on the mountain,
The shadowy forms of men and horses, looming, large-sized, flickering,
And over all the sky—the sky! far, far out of reach, studded, breaking out, the
    eternal stars.

Walt Whitman (1819-1892), "Bivouac on a Mountain Side"

When I get home I shall be qualified for any position, either that of boot black, a cleaner of brasses, a washer-(wo)man, cook, chambermaid, hewer of wood & drawer of water, or, failing in all these I can turn beggar & go from door to door asking for "broken vittles." In all these I should feel perfectly at home by long practise therein.

> Samuel Storrow, Union soldier from Massachusetts,
> December 4, 1862

I shan't feel at home out of the Army. I shall wake up in the morning and want to know if the drums have beaten and be asking for a pass when I want to go up town.

> C. B. Thurston, Union soldier from Maine,
> on why he will re-enlist, March 30, 1863

Sand flies, midges, mosquitoes, stinging ants, little red ticks . . . leave very little of us.

> John Appleton, Union lieutenant, June 1863

Oh hasten, then, that glorious day,
When buglers shall no longer play,
When we through peace shall be set free,
From "Tattoo," "Taps," and "Reveille."

> Confederate soldier song

You are liking the place so well and seem to enjoy a soldier's life so much I do not know but there is some danger of your liking it so well you will not care anything about living with me any more. Do you think there is?

> Harriet Jane Thompson, letter to "My own dear William"

Mary Jackson is my name
Single is my station
Happy will be the soldier boy—
Who makes the alteration.

> Note attached to a quilt sent to Union troops

We cook and eat, talk and laugh with the enemy's dead lying all about us as though they were so many hogs.

> Samuel T. Foster, Confederate captain, Texas brigade

I am bare footed.

> George Woodward, Confederate soldier from North Carolina,
> letter to his brother, December 27, 1863

I must say that I feel down in the mouth, only paid a week ago and have not a cent now, having bluffed away all that I did not send home. I don't think I will play poker any more.

> Jacob E. Hyneman, Union soldier under General Grant,
> February 20, 1864

The common private soldier earns enough in one month to buy a pretty fair watermelon.

> T. P. Forrester, Confederate soldier
> from Georgia, September 11, 1864

Reduced to the minimum, the private soldier consisted of one man, one hat, one jacket, one shirt, one pair of pants, one pair of drawers, one pair of shoes, and one pair of socks. His baggage was one blanket, one rubber blanket, and one haversack.

> Confederate soldier, 1865

Officers and Their Men

[Lewis] wore uniform & carried a sword & carbine & road & scouted & skirmished & fought like the rest.

A reflection on Maria Lewis, African American
woman soldier who fought with the 8th New York Cavalry

He said it was mighty hard for white folk now. He said he had quit carrying a pass and his master had just commenced to carry them.

C. E. Taylor, Confederate sergeant,
reporting to his father what an African American
in Mississippi said after witnessing a guard
demand to see Taylor's pass, July 1861

Our men are not good soldiers. They brag, but don't perform, complain sadly if they don't get everything they want, and a march of a few miles uses them up. It will take a long time to overcome these things, and what is in store for us in the future I know not.

William T. Sherman, Union general,
after the first Battle of Bull Run, 1861

"We'll pray for the privates, the noblest of all:
They do all the work and get no glory at all.
May good luck and good fortune them always attend!"
"And return crowned with laurels!" said the Soldier's Amen.

"The Soldier's Amen"

Glory is not for the private soldier, such as die in the hospitals, being eat up with the deadly gangrene, and being imperfectly waited on. Glory is for generals, colonels, majors, captains, and lieutenants.

Sam Watkins, Confederate private from Tennessee

I was severe, but endeavored to be just, for I knew if we could not command our men, we had no business to attempt invasion.

William T. Sherman, Union general,
on disciplining Union troops

Q.—What is the first duty of a Captain?
A. —To forget all the promises he made to the boys when he was elected, and put on dignified airs in the presence of his old associates.
Q. —What is the second duty?
A. —To get a finer uniform than his Colonel.
Q. —What is the third duty?
A. —To become the best poker player in the army.

From "Military Catechism,"
written for the soldier paper *The Army Argus*,
but published in the Mobile *Register*, 1862

The road to glory cannot be followed with much baggage.

Richard Ewell, Confederate general,
to his soldiers, May 1862

We enlisted to put down the rebellion, and had no patience with the red-tape tom-foolery of the regular service . . . A private was ready at the drop of a hat to thrash his commander; a feat that occurred more than once.

Union private from Indiana

I am of the opinion that married soldiers should be given the opportunity of embracing their families at least once a year, their places in the ranks taken by unmarried men. The population must not be allowed to suffer.

Reported by English observer Sir Arthur James Lyon Fremantle
to be a "very popular" item in the manifesto of a
General Chambers, candidate for the governor of Texas, 1863

I yield to no man in sympathy, but I am obliged to sweat these men tonight so I may save their blood tomorrow.

Stonewall Jackson, Confederate general,
replying to a colonel who was pressing him to rest his men

Good soldiers are never flogged, and there is no more hardship or disgrace to them in bad ones being thus punished than there is to good people in murderers being hanged.

Austrian captain Fitzgerald Ross, 1865

Johnny Reb on Billy Yank

Among the privates, the greed for gain, and the object with which they fight was not concealed in the slightest degree. They spoke in raptures of the capacity of Mississippi's soil for white labor, and declared their intention to get a grant of land from the United States and settle there after the war is over.

Alexander St. Clair Abrams, ex-Confederate soldier and reporter,
on the fall of Vicksburg, July 4, 1863

Yankee soldiers are very much like ships: to move them, you must "slush the ways."

Anthony Keiley, Confederate officer and prisoner of war,
on the bribability of his hosts at Point Lookout,
Maryland, 1864

You for one have met your just reward, which is a grant of land from the Confederates of three feet by six, in an obscure spot, where your friends if you have any, will never be able to find your body, for there is nothing to mark the spot except a small hillock of red clay, which a few hard rains will wash away.

J. C. Salter, Confederate soldier,
addressing the grave of a Union soldier, July 11, 1864

They talk about the ravages of the enemy in their marches through the country, but I do not think that the Yankees are any worse than our own army.

William Nugent, Confederate soldier, September 1864

Our barbarous foes are not entirely lost to all the dictates, and impulses of humanity. Would to God that the exhibition of it were more frequent in their occurrence.

George McDonnell,
on the burning of Atlanta, November 4, 1864

What's the use of killing Yankees? You kill one and six appear in his place.

Confederate soldier, late in the war

I forgive you. I know you are deluded.

R. M. Campbell, Confederate soldier,
note in his diary to the Northern soldier
into whose hands it might fall if he were killed

Billy Yank on Johnny Reb

The greatest enemy that we have to contend with here at present is secesh in ladies apparel.

George Smith Avery, Union soldier from Palmyra,
Missouri, referring to Confederate president Jefferson Davis
in a letter to his future wife

To give you an idea of Southern love for titles, I'll name part of the citizens who help to form our party next Wednesday. Colonel Cobb, Colonel Provinse,

Colonel Young, and Majors Hall and Hust. Every man who owns as many as
two negroes is at least a colonel. None of them rank as low as captains.

Charles W. Wills, Union soldier in Alabama,
Army Life of an Illinois Soldier

I pity the poor devils and still I cannot help hating them.

Hamlin Alexander Coe, Union sergeant in Tennessee,
on Confederate deserters

Give those South Carolina villians h—l and we will support you.

Member of the 7th Regiment National Guard,
letter to U.S. president Abraham Lincoln, April 10, 1861

I must lie to rebels, steal from rebels and kill rebels—Uncle Sam making vic-
arious atonement for these sins.

John F. Holahan, Union soldier, November 3, 1862

The rebels cannot increase their forces in the field. They already have out every
available man, and great numbers of conscripts are worthless as soldiers from
physical infirmities. I have seen men with hollow chests . . . and some even with
but one Arm, men with an eye gone and a great many already worthless from
general debility—and feeble constitutions, fit only for the Hospitals.

Neal Dow, Union general, prisoner of war in Richmond,
letter to Abraham Lincoln, November 12, 1863

They aimed better than our men; they covered themselves (in case of need)
more carefully and effectively; they could move in a swamp without much
care for alignment and touch of elbow. In short, they fought more like red-
skins or like hunters than we.

J. W. DeForest, Union veteran and novelist,
on the Army of Northern Virginia

Braver men never shouldered a musket.

Union soldier from Wisconsin,
of the Confederate army under General Johnston,
during the Atlanta campaign, 1864

Interaction

"Who are you?"

"We are two men of the Twelth Georgia, carrying a wounded comrade to the hospital."

"Don't you know you are in the Union lines?'

"No."

"You are. Go to your right."

"Man, you've got a heart in you."

Exchange between a Union sentry and Confederate soldiers,
at the second Battle of Bull Run, August 1862,
from a clipping in Confederate Veteran

Federals, respect my father's corpse.

Penciled note left on the body of a uniformed
Confederate officer at the Battle of Shiloh,
according to a Union officer, The Civil War in Song & Story

"Hant you got no better clothes than those?"

"You are a set of damned fools—do you suppose we put on our good clothes to go out to kill damned dogs?"

Exchange between a Union soldier and Confederate private
Tom Martin at the siege of Atlanta, November 1862

They are afraid we will get to think and won't fight.

Numa Barned, Union soldier, reporting why Union commanders
forbade their men to talk to Confederate soldiers,
December 27, 1862

They are sick and tired and if we will stack arms and go home they will do the same and hang their Ringleaders.

> Numa Barned, Union soldier, reporting what
> Confederate soldiers told him and
> his fellow troops, December 27, 1862

Knives spoons pipes money and most everything.

> Numa Barned, Union soldier, reporting what was swapped
> between soldiers of both sides near Falmouth, Virginia,
> December 27, 1862

Reb: What makes your folks leave us so many good clothes and fine blankets? Yank: We obey the injunction to clothe the naked and feed the hungry.

> Exchange at Fredericksburg, December 1862,
> *History of the Second Regiment New Hampshire Volunteers*

We send you some Tobacco by our Packet. Send us some coffee in return. Also a deck of cards if you have them, and we will send you more tobacco. Send us any late papers if you have them.

> Jas. O. Parker, Confederate soldier,
> note addressed to "Gents U.S. Army," attached to
> a "miniature boat six inches long," and floated down
> the Rappahannock to a New Jersey regiment, 1863

If the settlement of this war was left to the Enlisted men of both sides we would soon go home.

> James K. Newton, Union soldier,
> reporting the general opinion of soldiers from both armies,
> who discussed the matter together outside of Vicksburg,
> Summer 1863

Reb: When is Grant going to march into Vicksburg?
Yank: When you get your last mule and dog eat up.

Exchange at Vicksburg, July 1863,
recorded by M. Ebeneezer Wescott

You could not stand up day after day in those indecisive contests where over-whelming victory was impossible because neither side would run as they ought when beaten without getting at least something of the same brother-hood for the enemy that the north pole of a magnet has for the south.

Oliver Wendell Holmes Jr.

We made a bargain with them that we would not fire on them if they would not fire on us, and they were as good as their word. It seems too bad that we have to fight men that we like.

Union soldier under General Sherman,
of a friendly meeting with Confederate soldiers, 1864

'Mid pleasures and palaces though I may roam,
Be it ever so humble, there's no place like home.
A charm from the sky seems to hallow us there,
Which, seek thro' the world, is ne'er met with elsewhere.
Home! Home! Sweet, sweet home!
There's no place like home,
There's no place like home.

"Home, Sweet Home"

To Battle

Bang, bang, bang, a rattle, de bang, bang, bang, a boom, de bang . . . whirr-siz-siz-siz—a ripping, roaring, boom, bang!

Sam Watkins, Confederate private,
describing a "fire fight"

"The trouble was," said the old man, "I thought they were all shooting at me. Yes, sir, I thought every man in the other army was aiming at me in particular, and only me. And it seemed so darned unreasonable, you know. I wanted to explain to 'em what an almighty good fellow I was, because I thought then they might quit trying to hit me. But I couldn't explain, and they kept on being unreasonable—blim!—blam! bang! So I run!"

Stephen Crane, "The Veteran"

It was eyes right, guide center! Close-up, guide right, halt, forward, right oblique, left oblique, halt, forward, guide center, eyes right, dress up promptly in the rear, steady, double quick, charge bayonets, fire at will, is about all that a private soldier knows of a battle.

Sam Watkins, Confederate private

I want to be in one Battle, just for the curiosity of the thing.

George M. Decherd, Confederate soldier, January 6, 1862

You have frequently heard of the wild excitement of battle. I experience no such feelings. There is a sense of depression continually working away at my heart, caused by a knowledge of the great suffering in store for large numbers of my fellow men.

William Nugent, Confederate soldier

We heard all through the war that the army "was eager to be led against the enemy." It must have been so, for truthful correspondents said so, and editors confirmed it. But when you came to hunt for this particular itch, it was always the next regiment that had it.

The truth is, when bullets are whacking against tree trunks and solid shot are cracking skulls like eggshells, the consuming passion in the breast of the average man is to get out of the way.

David Thompson, Union soldier from New York

There was men laying wanting help, wanting water, with blood running out them and the top or sides their heads gone, great big holes in them . . . I just wants to git back to that old plantation and pick more cotton.

Thomas Cole, ex-slave and reluctant soldier
from Alabama

I have bin in one battle and that satisfied me with war and I would beg to be excused next time.

Habun R. Foster, Confederate soldier from Virginia,
July 26, 1862

In the charge I saw one soldier falter repeatedly, bowing as if before a hurricane. He would gather himself together, gain his place in the ranks, and again drop behind. Once or twice he fell to his knees, and at last he sank to the ground, still gripping his musket and bowing his head. I lifted him to his feet and said, "Coward!" . . . His pale distorted face flamed. He flung at me, "You lie!" Yet he didn't move; he couldn't; his legs would not obey him.

Albert R. Small, Union soldier,
on the Battle of Fredericksburg, December 13, 1862

If men were not afraid to die it would simplify matters very much. They are afraid & fear makes them run.

Oliver O. Howard, Union general

After the first round the fear left me, & I was as cool as ever I was in my life. I think I have been a great deal more excited in attempting to speak a piece in school or to make remarks at an evening meeting.

Herbert E. Valentine, Union soldier, January 2, 1863

If you should go with us to the battle filed and see those that are so gay thier faces pale and thier nervs tremblings and see an ankziety on every countenance almost bordering on fear, you would be very apt to think we were all a set of cowardly poltrouns.

> James T. Miller, Union soldier, May 24, 1863

In many instances arms and legs and sometimes heads protrude and my attention has been directed to several places where the hogs were actually rooting out the bodies and devouring them.

> David Wills, banker and civic leader,
> on the Gettysburg battlefield, three weeks after
> the battle, letter to Governor Andrew Curtin, July 24, 1863

I never did git to where I wasn't scared when we goes into the battle. This the last one I's in, and I's sure glad, for I never seed the like of dead and wounded men.

> Thomas Cole, ex-slave and soldier from Alabama,
> on the Missionary Ridge battle in Tennessee, November 1863

Sometimes it looked like the war was about to cut my ears off. I would lay stretched out on the ground and bullets would fly over my head. I would take a rock and place it on top of my head, thinking maybe it would keep the bullet from going through my brain.

> African American soldier

Abraham Lincoln observed the battle of Fort Stevens, taking an exposed position on a parapet until a young lieutenant colonel who didn't recognize him yelled, "Get down, you damn fool, before you get shot." The lieutenant colonel was Oliver Wendell Holmes Jr., the future Supreme Court justice.

> *USA Today*, January 12, 1996

Do they miss me in the trench, do they miss me?
When the shells fly so thickly around?
Do they know that I've run down the hillside
To look for my hole in the ground?
But the shells exploded so near me,
It seemed best for me to run;
And though some laughted as I crawfished,
I could not discover the fun.

"Do They Miss Me in the Trenches?"
a parody of the sentimental war song,
"Do They Miss Me at Home?"

Just before the battle, mother,
I was drinking mountain dew,
When I saw the "Rebels" marching,
To the rear I quickly flew;
Where the stragglers were flying,
Thinking of their homes and wives;
'Twas not the "Reb" we feared, dear mother,
But our own dear precious lives.

Chorus: Farewell, mother! for you'll never
See my name among the slain.
For if I only can skedaddle,
Dear mother, I'll come home again.

"Farewell Mother," parody of the sentimental
war song, "Just Before the Battle, Mother"

Unnamed, unknown, remain and still remain the bravest soldiers. Our manliest,
our boys, our hardy darlings: no picture gives them. Likely, the typical one of
them (standing, no doubt, for hundreds, thousands) crawls aside to some bush-
clump or ferny tuft on receiving his death-shot; there, sheltering a little while,
soaking roots, grass, and soil with red blood; the battle advances, retreats, flits
from the scene, sweeps by; and there, haply with pain and suffering . . . the last
lethargy winds like a serpent round him; the eyes glaze in death; . . . and there, at
last, the Bravest Soldier, crumbles in Mother Earth, unburied and unknown.

Walt Whitman, March 27, 1865

Confederate camp, Warrington Navy Yard, Pensacola, Florida, 1861

Food and Drink

Thus we swallow politics with every meal. We take a mouthful and read a telegram, one eye on the table, the other on the paper. One must be made of cool stuff to keep calm and collected, but I say but little. The war has banished small talk. Through all this black servants move about quietly, never seeming to notice that this is all about them.

G., a pro-Union woman from New Orleans,
diary entry, March 10, 1861

They surrounded our wells like the locusts of Egypt and struggled with each other for the water as if perishing with thirst, and they thronged our kitchen doors and windows, begging for bread like hungry wolves.

Shaker community manuscript journal,
describing the soldiers of Humphrey Marshall's
Confederate brigade passing through their Kentucky settlement

Q.—What is the first duty of the commissary?
A.—To take all the delicacies provided by the army for his own use.
Q.—What is the second duty?
A.—To share sparingly said delicacies with his friends, and never let them go into such vulgar places as the mouths of sick soldiers.
Q.—What is the third duty?
A.—To be very particular to see that the requisitions for rations are in proper form—all the t's crossed and i's dotted—when presented by soldiers who are sick or who have had nothing to eat for three or for days.

> From "Military Catechism,"
> written for the soldier paper *The Army Argus*,
> but published in the Mobile *Register*, 1862

I profess to be a Christian, and my bible teaches me if my enemy hungers to feed him—if he is thirsty to give him drink.

> Amy Bradley, Union nurse,
> retort to a doctor's warning not to care so
> assiduously for a Confederate soldier, June 1862

I fear this liquor more than Pope's army.

> Stonewall Jackson, Confederate general,
> instructing a captain to pour out barrels of whiskey
> found in a confiscated warehouse, August 1862

Whiskey is a monster, and ruins great and small,
But in our noble army, Headquarters gets it all;
They drink it when there's danger, although it seems too hard,
But if a private touches it they put him "under guard."

> "The Brass-Mounted Army," a soldiers' song

The hard bread is all worms and the meat stinks like hell . . . and rice to or three times a week & worms as long as your finger. I liked rice once but god damn the stuff now.

> H. Holden, Union soldier, August 30, 1862

Last evening a new brigadier-general, aged ninety-four years, made a speech to Regiment Five, Mackerel Brigade, and then furnished each man with a lead-pencil. He said that, as the Government was disappointed about receiving some provisions it had ordered for the troops, those pencils were intended to enable them to draw their rations as usual.

Robert H. Newell, humorist,
The Orpheus C. Kerr Papers, 1862–1871

We live on crackers so hard that if we loaded our guns with them we could of killed seceshs in a hurry.

Union private from Illinois

If I ever lose my patriotism, and the "secesh" spirit dies out, then you may know the "Commissary" is at fault. Corn meal mixed with water and tough beef three times a day will knock the "Brave Volunteer" under quicker than Yankee bullets.

Robert P. Banks, Confederate private, October 22, 1862

Our generals eat the poultry, and buy it very cheap,
Our colonels and our majors devour the hog and sheep;
The privates are contented (except when they can steal),
With beef and corn bread plenty to make a hearty meal.

"The Brass-Mounted Army," a soldiers' song

Reduce our rations at all?
It was difficult, yet it was done—
We had one meal a day—it was small—
Are we now, oh ye gods, to have none?
Oh, ye gentlemen issuing rations,
Give at least half her own to the State,
Put a curb on your maddening passions,
And commissaries—commiserate!

"Short Rations,"
a song dedicated to "The Corn-Fed Army of Tennessee"

Now the good people will remember us, for we spared them the trouble, in a good many instances, of feeding the corn to their turkeys and chickens, which they may need before this cruel war is over.

D. G. Crotty, Union soldier from Michigan,
on why it was a favor to the Southerners
to "gobble up" their turkeys

Whereas, The matter of provisions is a great expense to the United States of America, besides offering inducements for unexpected raids on the part of the famishing foeman; the Mackerel Brigade is hereby directed to live entirely upon the Southern Confederacy, eating him alive wherever found, and partaking of no other food.

Robert H. Newell, humorist,
The Orpheus C. Kerr Papers, 1862–1871

Q.—What is the first duty of the surgeon?
A.—Under the names of drugs and medicines, to purchase a full supply of good liquors.
Q.—What is the second duty?
A.—To cause all private cellars to be searched, and all the good brandies found there to be confiscated, lest the owners should smuggle them to the soldiers, give them away and make the whole army drunk.
Q.—What is the third duty?
A.—To see that he and his assistants drink up all of said liquors.

from "Military Catechism,"
written for the soldier paper *The Army Argus,*
but published in the Mobile *Register,* 1862

These cookies are expressly for the sick soldiers, and if anybody else eats them, I hope they will choke him!

Note attached to a box of cookies sent to Union troops

I wish this war was over, when, free from rags and fleas,
We'd kiss our wives and sweethearts and gobble goober peas.
Peas! Peas! Peas! eating goober peas!
Goodness, how delicious, eating goober peas!

Popular Confederate war song

Dear mother, I remember well,
The food we get from Uncle Sam:
Hard tack, salt fish, and rusty pork,
Sometimes a scanty piece of ham.
When I a furlough did receive,
I bade adieu to Brother Pete—
Oh, mother, for a plate of hash,
DEAR MOTHER, I'VE COME HOME TO EAT!

Popular soldier parody of the song,
"Dear Mother, I've Come Home to Die"

One cup of coffee each (which is the staff of life for a soldier), two pieces of
fried pork (the last we had) and four crackers a piece and each cracker contained from ten to thirty worms varying in length from ⅛ to ½ an inch . . . We
broke them into our coffee to scald them and dipped them out with a spoon
as they came squirming to the top.

Perry Mayo, Union soldier,
describing his Thanksgiving dinner, December 1, 1862

On the doorsteps sat the young mother, beautiful in desolation, with a baby
in her arms, and on either side of her a little one, piteously crying for something to eat. "Oh, mama, I want something to eat, so bad." "Oh, mama, I am
so hungry—give me something to eat." Thus the children were begging for
what the mother had not to give.

Mary A. H. Gay, Life in Dixie During the War 1861–1865

We are utterly cut off from the world, surrounded by a circle of fire . . . People do nothing but eat what then can get, sleep when they can, and dodge the shells . . . I think all the dogs and cats must be killed or starved. We don't see anymore pitiful animals prowling around.

Young woman's diary entry,
on the siege of Vicksburg, May 22–July 4, 1863

For forty miles there is not an ear of corn and scarcely a cow or a hog. Little children cry for bread, and gaunt famine with a visage of misery and want flies like a destroying angel over the land.

George Chittenden, Union soldier,
letter to his wife Amanda, July 25, 1863

I confess I never saw so much universal profusion, and, I may say, waste. Hot meats and cold meats, venison pies, fish, oysters . . . eggs, boiled, poached, "scrambled," and in omelettes, hot rolls and cakes, several kinds of bread, fruit in season, &c., &c., are served up for breakfast, with "Confederate" (i.e., artificial) coffee and tea . . . in quantities sufficient to satisfy an army of hungry soldiers . . . The country is evidently very far from the starvation which the Yankees so charitably reckon upon as one of their chief auxiliaries in destroying the population of the South.

Austrian captain Fitzgerald Ross,
describing Richmond, December 1863

Talking about Hasheesh I mean to get you to let me make some long wished for experiments with that Drug—For the benefit of Science you know.

Ned Hormons, Union soldier from New York City,
letter to his fiancée, January 9, 1864

Next to the Yankeys Comes Rations which most interest a Soldier.

Jerome Yates, Confederate private from Virginia,
January 1864

I had to steal my food; took turkeys, chickens and pigs; before I left our number had increased to thirty, of whom ten were women; we were four miles in the rear of the plantation house; sometimes we would rope beef cattle and drag them out to our hiding place.

> Corporal Octave Johnson, testimony before
> American Freedmen's Inquiry Commission about his running away
> from his New Orleans slavemaster, February 1864

Hunger to starving men is totally unrelated to the desire for food as that is commonly understood and felt. It is a great agony of the whole body and of the soul as well. It is unimaginable, all-pervading pain inflicted when the strength to endure pain is entirely gone.

> George Cary Eggleston, Confederate sergeant from Virginia,
> on the starvation of Confederate troops, June 1864

The idea that there is plenty for all in the country is absurd. The efforts of the enemy have been too successful . . . people have killed whole flocks of sheep, breeding stock of cattle and young cattle.

> Lucius Northrup, Confederate commissary general,
> December 20, 1864

I could not be oblivious to the fact that I was hungry, very hungry. And there was another, whose footsteps were becoming more and more feeble day by day and whose voice, when heard at all, was full of the pathos of despair, who needed nourishment that could not be obtained, and consolation, which it seemed a mockery to offer.

> Mary Gay, Decatur, Georgia,
> on her and her mother's starvation
> after the siege of Atlanta

It must be a matter of gratitude as well as surprise, for our people to see a Government which was lately fighting us with fire, and sword, and shell, now generously feeding our poor and distressed . . . Again, the Confederate soldier, with one leg or one arm, the crippled, maimed, and broken, and the worn and destitute men, who fought bravely their enemies then, their benefactors now, have their sacks filled and are fed.

Southern reporter, on government aid in Atlanta, 1865

Wish I had been taught to cook instead of how to play on the piano. A practical knowledge of the preparation of food products would stand me in better stead at this juncture than any amount of information regarding the scientific principles of music. I adore music, but I can't live without eating—and I'm hungry.

Malvina Black Gist, Confederate war widow,
suffering food shortages, Richmond, March 1865

Two days fasting, marching, and fighting was not uncommon . . . The men subsisted on corn intended for the battery horses, raw bacon captured from the enemy, and the water of springs, creeks, and rivers.

Confederate soldier,
of the retreat to Appomattox, April 1865

A Southern family

Women and the War

I was served might mean before the Yankees came here. I was nearly frostbitten: my old Missus made me weave to make clothes for the [Confederate] soldiers till 12 o'clock at night & I was so tired & my own clothes I had to spin over night. She never gave me so much as a bonnet. I had to work hard for the rebels until the very last day when they took us.

Nancy Johnson, former slave, Georgia,
in testimony, March 22, 1873

Ladies who never worked before are hard at work making uniforms and tents.

Catherine Ann Edmonston, North Carolina,
diary entry, May 3, 1861

That man . . . says that women need to be helped into carriages, and lifted over ditches, and to have the best place everywhere. Nobody ever helps me into carriages, or over mud puddles, or give me any best place, and aren't I a woman? . . . I have plowed, and planted, and gathered into barns, and no man could head me—and aren't I a woman? I could work as much and eat as much as a man (when I could get it), and bear the lash as well—and aren't I a woman? I have borne thirteen children and seen them most all sold off into slavery, and when I cried out with a mother's grief, none but Jesus heard—and aren't I a woman?

Sojourner Truth,
Women's Rights Convention, Ohio, 1854

Shall men come here and die by tens of thousands for us, and shall no woman be found to die for them?

Margaret Elizabeth Breckinridge, Confederate nurse,
who later died of a disease contracted in an army hospital

Youth is impulsive, and prone to run with the crowd. We caught the infection of the war spirit in the air and never stopped to reason or to think.

Eliza Frances Andrews, looking back on the suffering she,
a secessionist, imposed on her Unionist father

Of all the principles developed by the late war, I think the capability of our Southern women to take care of themselves by no means the least important.

Thomas Smith Dabney, letter to his daughter Emmy

I shall never get used to being left as the head of affairs at home. The burden is very heavy, and there is no one to smile on me as I trudge wearily along in the dark with it. I am constituted so as to crave a guide and protector, I am not an independent woman nor ever shall be.

Emily Harris, South Carolina

All my life I have shunned responsibility & have been so dependent on the love of my friends for happiness—now I am compelled to think & act for myself.

Louisa Brown Pearl, Nashville

I also said a man did not deserve the name of man, if he did not fight for his country; nor a woman, the name of woman, if she did not do all in her power to aid the men.

Kate Cumming, Georgia

"How manfully you stood by me!"
"How womanfully, you mean," she replied, smiling.

Exchange between a husband and wife,
in a story by abolitionist Lydia Maria Child, 1856

Oh if I could put some of my reckless spirit into these discreet, cautious, lazy men.

Mary Chesnut, April 1861

Go boys, to your country's call! I'd rather be a brave man's widow than a coward's wife.

Chanted by the women of Eucheeanna, Florida,
as they marched through town early in 1861

Husband gone to the army again, every thing resting on me, children troublesome, company forever, weather very cold, Negroes in the newground, cows, calves and sheep on the wheat.

Emily Harris, South Carolina

You must not call me a brave and contented girl, because I ain't one bit. And one thing more I want you to quit flourishing about over the hills and valleys when you are in the midst of so many secessionists. I know you are very brave an all that But I want you to do just as I tell you.

> Amanda Chittendon, to her husband George,
> a Union soldier, September 1861

I doubt if history affords a parallel to the deep and bitter enmity of the women of the South. No one who sees them and hears them but must feel the intensity of their hate.

> William T. Sherman, Union general, letter to his wife

The women of the South kept the war alive—and it is only by making them suffer that we can subdue the men.

> Jeremiah Jenkins, Union lieutenant colonel,
> replying to a Columbia woman who accused him
> of making war on women and children

So you're the little woman who wrote the book that made this great war!

> Abraham Lincoln, upon meeting Harriet Beecher Stowe

I think these times make all women feel their humiliation in the affairs of the world. With men it is one to the field—"glory, honour, praise, &c, power." Women can only stay at home—& every papers reminds us that women are to be violated—ravished & all manner of humiliation. How are the daughters of Eve punished.

> Mary Chesnut

There were few men in the city at this time; but the women of the South still fought their battle for them: fought it resentfully, calmly, but silently! Clad in their mourning garments, overcome but hardly subdued, they sat within their desolate homes, or if compelled to leave that shelter went on their errands to church or hospital with veiled faces and swift steps. By no sign or act did the possessors of their fair city know that they were even conscious of their presence.

Pheobe Pember, on life in occupied Richmond

The battle of Manassas robed many of our women in mourning, and some of those who had no graves to deck were weeping silently as they walked through the scented avenues.

G., a pro-Union woman from New Orleans,
on walking through a cemetery,
diary entry, November 10, 1861

Does anybody wonder so many women die? Grief and constant anxiety kill nearly as many women as men die on the battlefield.

Mary Chesnut

We shall with pleasing remembrance ever bear in mind that woman . . . with her fountain of affection, and lofty patriotism, though the weaker sex accomplishes as much in this momentous struggle for liberty as the marshaled hosts of our soldiery.

Frank N. Marks, Confederate officer, March 23, 1862

Now, when if ever man was stirred to the highest for his country & for his own future—he seems as utterly absorbed by Negro squabble, hay stealing, cotton saving . . . If I had been a man in this great revolution—I should have either been killed at once or made a name & done some good for my country.

Mary Chesnut, on her husband

I say, "Never, never, though we perish in the track of their endeavor." Words, idle words. What can poor weak women do?

Kate Stone, Louisiana,
advocating Southern resistance, late in the war

All in favor of resistance, no matter how hopeless that resistance might be.

Julia LeGrand, describing the mindset
of the women of New Orleans as to the impending
Union occupation, April 1862

The ladies of the place allow no opportunity to pass, to insult our soldiers & our flag. If I had the managing of the place I would burn the town.

S.J.F. Miller, Union soldier,
Huntsville, Alabama, July 1862

O! if I was only a man! Then I could don the breeches, and slay them with a will! If some few Southern women were in the ranks, they could set the men an example they would not blush to follow. Pshaw! there are no women here! We are all men!

Sarah Morgan, Baton Rouge

Had the women of the Confederacy lived in a more heroic age, in which their sex put on armor and went forth to battle with dignity, it is possible that they would have produced real Amazons and Joans of Arc.

F. B. Simkins and J. W. Patton

Oh, yes, I am a Southern girl,
And glory in the name,
And boast it with far greater pride
Than glittering wealth or fame.

We envy not the Northern girl,
Her robes of beauty rare,
Though diamonds grace her snowy neck,
And pearls bedeck her hair.

"The Homespun Dress"

The women here generally are shaped like a lath, nasty, slab-sided, long haired specimens of humanity. I would as soon kiss a dried codfish as one of them.

Henry S. Simmons, Union soldier,
letter to his wife, November 16, 1862

I sat down by a fire in company with three young women, all cleanly dressed, and powdered to death. Their ages were from 18 to 24. Each of them had a quid of tobacco in her cheek about the size of my stone inkstand, and if they didn't make the extract fly worse than I ever saw in any country grocery, shoot me.

Union captain from Illinois,
letter from Scottsboro, Alabama

We discovered last week a soldier who turned out to be a girl. She had already been in service for 21 months and was twice wounded. Maybe she would have remained undiscovered for a long time if she hadn't fainted. She was given a warm bath which gave the secret away.

Union cavalryman from Indiana, February 1863

I feel a deep & abiding interest in our female soldiers. They are patriots in the truest sense of the word, and I more than admire them.

Stonewall Jackson, Confederate general,
letter to Mary Tucker Magill

The ladies are so modest that they write of themselves with a little i . . .
Penmanship, spelling and composition showed that the greatest need of the
South is an army of Northern Schoolmasters.

> William Thompson Lusk, Union officer from Connecticut,
> of letters from Southerners that had fallen
> into Northern hands

Thoroughly educated women are deplorably rare among us.

> Augusta Jane Evans, Mobile,
> on Southern aristocracy, July 15, 1863

I think if we fight much longer we will come down as low as slaves, and I think
we had better give up, and have our husbands with us. Slavery if such it will be,
will be much harder when we are subdued after our husbands are killed.

> Octavia Stephens, Florida,
> letter to her husband, August 5, 1863

Some of the young ladies around Natchet are receiving attention from the
Yankees. I think it shows so little character not to resist love of admiration more.

> Kate Foster, Mississippi, September 20, 1863

John, Sarah & Rose have left and I did the washing for six weeks, came near
ruining myself for life as I was too delicately raised for such hard work.

> Kate Foster, Mississippi,
> on life without her slaves, November 15, 1863

At thirty-two I am as old as I ought to be at fifty.

> Martha Lamison, Unionist who had to flee
> her home in Missouri, November 29, 1863

Our patriotism is mainly in the army and among the ladies of the South.

> John B. Jones, clerk in the Confederate
> war department, December 1, 1863

I think the hearts of women suffer more real sorrow than those that are called to still their beating upon the battlefield. They are at rest and know no more pain; we are left [to] mourn their loss, and hide our anguish deep in our own hearts.

> Angie, fiancée of a Confederate soldier, June 9, 1864

I do not believe there is more than one woman in a thousand in the whole southern Confederacy who is virtuous, & the men are universally libertines.

> George Avery, Union soldier,
> camped in Little Rock, June 1864

Arise then, women of this day! Arise all women who have hearts, whether your baptism be that of water or of tears! Say firmly, "We will not have great questions decided by irrelevant agencies. Our husbands shall not come to us, reeking of carnage, for caresses and applause. Our sons shall not be taken from us to unlearn all that we have been able to teach them of charity, mercy and patience. We women of one country will be too tender of those of another country to allow our sons to be trained to injure theirs." From the bosom of the devastated earth a voice goes up with our own, it says, "Disarm! Disarm!"

> Julia Ward Howe, "Mother's Day Proclamation"

I cannot feel tho' any pleasure in hearing you say that you wish you were not a woman. The only solution of this country is in the hands of women not only now in all that they inspire men to do and bear and to believe in, or in the present help and aid they render to the country—but if ever this war does end it will be their part to restore order and to reform society.

> Harry Hammond, Confederate soldier,
> letter to his wife, August 19, 1864

It is high time I was having some experiences out of the ordinary, and if anything remarkable is going to happen, I want to know something about it; it might be worth relating to my grandchildren! Anyhow, it is frightfully monotonous, just because you are a woman, to be always tucked away in the safe places. I want to stay. I want to have a taste of danger.

> Malvina Black Gist, Confederate war widow,
> on the eve of moving from Columbia, South Carolina,
> to Richmond to escape Sherman's army, 1865

The people in parts of Georgia, Alabama & the Carolinas are ready to submit; but the real country is the army—it & the vast majority of the women are unconquered and unconquerable.

> William C. P. Breckinridge, Confederate officer,
> January 1865

We give up to the Yankees! How can it be? How can they talk about it? Why does not the President call out the women if there are [not] enough men? We would go and fight, too—we would better all die together.

> Emma LeConte, South Carolina, 1865

Most men dislike to admit that their wifes own anything. It is all the masculine "my" and "my own" which they use and in polite circles it would be considered in bad taste for a woman to say "my plantation," "my horse," "my cows" altho' they are really as much her own as the dress she wears.

> Ella Gertrude Clanton Thomas, June 19, 1869

Ghastly visions made night hideous. During the day, the quick galloping of a horse, the unexpected appearance of a visitor, would agitate a whole household, sending women in haste to some secret place where they might pray for strength to bear patiently whatever tidings the messenger should bring.

> Fannie Beers, nurse and wife
> of a Confederate soldier, 1888

I have never studied the art of paying compliments to women. But I must say that, if all that has been said by orators and poets since the creation of the world in praise of women was applied to the women of America, it would not do them justice for their conduct during the war.

Abraham Lincoln

Echoes

There was absolutely nothing which a man might possibly use that we did not make for them. We embroidered cases for razors, for soap and sponge, and cute morocco affairs for needles, thread, and court-plaster, with a little pocket lined with a bank-note. "How perfectly ridiculous!" do you say? Nothing is ridiculous that helps anxious women to bear their lot—cheats them with the hope that they are doing good.

Mrs. Roger Pryor, Reminiscences of War and Peace, 1904

Nobody was in sight but a poor thin country girl in a faded calico gown and sunbonnet. She stood alone on the platform, waiting. A child was playing beside her. When we stopped, the men took out from a freight car a rough, unplaned pine box and laid it down, baring their heads for a moment. Then the train steamed away. She sat down on the ground and put her arms around the box and leaned her head on it. The child went on playing.

Rebecca Harding Davis,
at a small train station in Pennsylvania, 1904

"[T]he foremost woman in America."

The Boston Transcript editor's description
of Mary Livermore, organizer of the
first Women's Suffrage Convention
in Chicago in 1868 and the Illinois chairperson
of the Woman Suffrage Association,
upon her death in 1905

Wounded at Fredericksburg

The Sick and the Wounded

It may seem a strange principle to enunciate as the very first requirement in a Hospital that it should do the sick no harm.

Florence Nightingale, *Notes on Hospitals*, 1859

I hear now of acres of dead and cities full of wounded with less sensibility than was at first occasioned by hearing of the loss of half a dozen men in a skirmish. As blow after blow falls, and our hearts are in a measure seared by the constant touch of the fire, we grow graver and older, and take a shock more quietly than we would have taken a trifling annoyance a year ago.

Mrs. Henry Dulaney

I am up to my neck in work. It is slaughter, slaughter, slaughter.

John Gardner Perry, Union surgeon

The crush'd head I dress, (poor crazed hand tear not the bandage away,)
The neck of the cavalry-man with the bullet through and through I examine,
Hard the breathing rattles, quite glazed already the eye, yet life struggles hard,
(Come sweet death! be persuaded O beautiful death!
In mercy come quickly.)

Walt Whitman (1819-1892), "The Wound Dresser"

When a person is sick in camp they might as well dig a hole and put him in
as to take him to one of the infernal hells called hospitals.

Albinus Fell, Union soldier,
letter to his wife, January 19, 1862

Our doctor knows about as much as a ten year old boy.

Edward W. Crippin, Union soldier from Illinois

The part to which leeches are to be applied should be carefully cleansed with
soap and water, and dried. The leeches will be made more active by putting
them in fresh water just before applying them. They may be applied by means
of a wineglass or pill-box, or by placing them in a clean napkin to be laid over
the part. Should they refuse to bit, the skin may be moistened with a little
milk, or pricked so as to draw blood.

Manual of Directions for Nurses in the Army Hospitals

Open the envelope quickly,
O this is not our son's writing, yet his name is sign'd,
O a strange hand writes for our dear son, O stricken mother's soul!
All swims before her eyes, flashes with black, she catches the main words only,

Sentences broken, gunshot wound in the breast, cavalry skirmish, taken
to hospital,
At present low, but will soon be better . . .

Alas poor boy, he will never be better, (nor may-be needs to be better, that
brave and simple soul,)
While they stand at home at the door he is dead already,
The only son is dead.

Walt Whitman (1819-1892), "Come Up from the Fields Father"

There comes that odious Walt Whitman to talk evil and unbelief to my boys
. . . I think I would rather see the Evil One himself.

Union nurse, letter to her husband

The better born—that is, those born in the purple, the gentry—were the better patients. They endure in silence.

Mrs. McCord, Columbia, South Carolina,
hospital volunteer

My satisfaction in visiting at the hospital has more than once been destroyed
by my going by mistake to a Yankee and giving him a delicacy prepared by
my own hands, which was so needed and would have been enjoyed by the
poor true Confederate who cast long eyes from the next bed.

Grace Elmore, Columbia, South Carolina,
hospital volunteer

Death in every awful form, if it really be death, is a pleasant sight in comparison to the fearfully and mortally wounded. Some crying, oh, my wife, my
children, others, my Mother, my sisters, my brother, etc. any and all of these
you will hear while some pray to God to have mercy and others die cursing
the "Yankee sons of b——s."

Andrew Devilbliss, Confederate soldier,
after the Battle of Shiloh, April 16, 1862

If a man Lives he Lives and if he Dies he Dies . . . A Dog is thought more of Down in Marion than a Solger is hear.

John Hall, Confederate soldier from Marion, Alabama,
writing from a hospital in Richmond, May 15, 1862

Our Regimental doctor has no more respect for a sick soldier than I would have for a good dog; no not near so much, for if my dog was sick or wounded I would spend some little time in relieving him. Our doctor will not.

William N. Price, Union soldier from Illinois,
One Year in the War

I thought of more things in one hour than I could write down in a year. I thought of a home far away . . . I wondered if my fate would ever be known to them. I had a horror of dying alone . . . I was afraid that none of my regiment would ever find me, and that with the unknown dead who lay scattered around me I would be buried in one common ground . . . How I longed for day. Just that some one might see me die.

E. D. Patterson, Confederate private,
wounded in battle, August 1862

I can truly say, that there is no position in the world that a woman can occupy, no matter how high or exalted it may be, for which I would exchange the one I have. And no happiness which any thing earthly could give, could compare with the pleasure I have experienced in receiving the blessings of the suffering and dying.

Kate Cumming, Confederate nurse

I could not help thinking how ridiculous our world must appear to superior intelligences—our incurring so much trouble, expense and suffering to maim and murder each other and after accomplishing this object, laying the poor creatures side by side—endeavoring to relieve their pain and save their lives.

Ann R. L. Schaeffer, recalling a visit to a Union hospital
after Antietam, September 1862

Death is nothing here. As you step out in the morning from your tent to wash your face, you see before you on a stretcher a shapeless, extended object, and over it is thrown a dark gray blanket. It is the corpse of some wounded or sick soldier of the regiment who died in the hospital tent during the night; perhaps there is a row of three or four of these corpses lying covered over. No one makes an ado.

Walt Whitman, December 26, 1862

Q.—What is the first duty of a Medical Director?
A.—To permit the sick and the wounded to take care of themselves.
Q.—What is the second duty?
A.—To learn the sick and wounded to be of little trouble to the medical department, and to this end to constantly ship those mortally wounded, or in extremis, to distant points, without attendants, and without anything to eat or drink.
Q.—What is the third duty?
A.—To employ a good part of his time in cursing the physician, in charge of those distant hospitals, for letting so many of the sick and wounded die.

From "Military Catechism,"
written for the soldier paper The Army Argus,
but published in the Mobile Register, 1862

I would like first rate to get such a wound . . . Oh! wouldn't it be nice to get a 30 days leave and go home and be petted like a baby, and get delicacies to eat . . . and then if I ever run for a little office I could limp and complain of the "old wound."

E. J. Ellis, Confederate soldier from Louisiana,
on a slight wound suffered by a fellow soldier,
March 18, 1863

Though we enlisted to fight and die, nothing happened to us so serious as the measles.

Union soldier of the 1st Maine,
on one of the greatest killers in the Civil War

I had rather risk a battle than the Hospitals.

> John Crosby, Union soldier, May 1, 1863

When I was carried into the building and looked about I could not help com-
paring the surgeons to fiends. It was dark & the building lighted partially with
candles: all around on the ground lay the wounded men; some of them were
shrieking, some cursing & swearing & some praying; in the middle of the room
was some 10 or 12 tables just large enough to lay a man on; these were used as
dissecting tables & they were covered with blood; near & around the tables
stood the surgeons with blood all over them & by the side of the tables was a
heap of feet, legs & arms.

> T. D. Kingsley, Union colonel,
> of a hospital in Baton Rouge, June 25, 1863

Swamp fever has turned our fine regiment into a sickly, dispirited, undisci-
plined wreck . . . Forty-two deaths in forty-two days; barely two hundred and
twenty-five men left for duty; and most of those staggering skeletons covered
with fever sores.

> J. W. DeForest, Union veteran and novelist,
> *A Volunteer's Adventures*, August 1863

A lady's respectability must be at a low ebb when it can be endangered by
going into a hospital.

> Kate Cumming, Confederate nurse,
> complaining about women who were slow to volunteer
> at hospitals on the grounds of respectability, September 1863

The army was in a bad way. Insufficiently sheltered, and continually drenched
with rain, the men were seldom able to dry their clothes; and a great deal of
sickness was the natural consequence.

> Austrian captain Fitzgerald Ross,
> describing an 1863 visit to the Confederate camp
> near Chickamauga, 1865

The surgeon insisted on Sending me to the hospital for treatment. I insisted on taking the field and prevailed—thinking that I had better die by rebel bullets than Union Quackery.

M. F. Roberts, Union soldier from Ohio, May 3, 1864

The doctors, of course, are doing much, and some are doing their full duty, but the majority are not. They have free access to the hospital stores and deem their own health demands that they drink up most of the brandy and whiskey in stock, and, being fired up most of the time, display a cruel and brutal indifference to the needs of the suffering.

Susan Lee Bickford, Virginia volunteer
in the Women's Relief Society, on a makeshift hospital
where she volunteered, May 12, 1864

[W]e are Deprived of the most importances things we Need in health and sickness Both That surficint Food and quality. As for The sick it is A shocking thing to Look into thire conditions. Death must Be thire Doom when once they have to go to the Hospital Never Return Again such is the medical Assistance of the 20th Rig [of New York].

George Rodgers, Thomas Sipple, and Samuel Sampson,
African American soldiers camped in New Orleans,
August 1864

The females . . . go gawking through the wards, peeping into every curtained couch, seldom exchanging a word with the occupant, but (as they invariably "hunt in couples") giving vent to their pent up "feelinks" in heart-rending (?) outbursts of "Oh, my Savior!" "Phoebe, do look here!" "Only see what a horrid wound!" "Goodness, gracious, how terrible war is!" "my! my!! my!!! Oh, let's go—I can't stand it any longer!" And as they near the door, perhaps these dear creatures will wind up with an audible—"Heavens! what a smell!"

Union soldier from Indiana,
on a Washington hospital, 1864

I do not suffer under the sights; but oh! the sounds, the screams of men.

Katharine Wormeley, nurse from Rhode Island,
The Other Side of War with the Army of the Potomac, 1889

No woman under thirty years need apply to serve in government hospitals. All nurses are required to be very plain looking women. Their dresses must be brown or black, with no bows, no curls, no jewelry and no hoop skirts.

Dorothea Dix, Union superintendent of female nurses

Echoes

That leg must come off—save a leg—lose the life.

S. Weir Mitchell, words spoken from his deathbed
that demonstrate the psychological impact of his time spent
as a wartime physician, 1913

We operated in old blood-stained and often pus-stained coats, the veterans of a hundred fights . . . We used undisinfected instruments from undisinfected plush-lined cases, and still worse, used marine sponges which had been used in prior pus cases and had been only washed in tap water. If a sponge or an instrument fell on the floor, it was washed and squeezed in a basin of tap water and used as if it were clean.

Surgeon in the Union army, looking back from World War I

[M]aimed and shattered survivors from a hundred battlefields, diseased and disabled soldiers released from hostile prisons, anguished and hopeless wives and mothers, made so by the slaughter of those who were dearest to them, [who] have found, many of them, temporary relief from their suffering in opium.

Horace Day, on the opium addiction
that spread through the United States masking emotional
and mental scars, quoted in
Opiate Addiction as a Consequence of the Civil War, 1978

Andersonville Prison, Georgia, August 17, 1864

Prisons and Prisoners of War

When at Wagner I was captured,
Then my courage failed;
Now I'm dirty, hungry, naked,
Here in Charleston Jail.

> "Down in Charleston Jail," prisoners' song

Its huge doors swung open and we were in the presence of—I do not know
what to call them. It was evident they were human beings but hunger, sickness, exposure and dirt had so transformed them that they more resembled
walking skeletons, painted black.

> Lucius Barber, Union sergeant under Sherman,
> on the Confederate prison at Andersonville

Painful as will be the necessity, this government will deal out to the prisoners held by it, the same treatment and the same fate as shall be experienced by those captured on the Savannah: and if driven to the terrible necessity of retaliation by your execution of any of the officers or crew of the Savannah, that retaliation will be extended so far as shall be requisite to secure abandonment by you of a practice unknown to the warfare of civilized man, and so barbarous as to disgrace the nation which shall be guilty of inaugurating it.

> Jefferson Davis, Confederate president,
> letter to Abraham Lincoln, on hearing reports that officers
> taken from the *C.S.S. Savannah* were being treated
> as criminals, July 6, 1861

They have been in prison for the Crime of Coming to Washington to reside, ever since about the fourth of April 1862 now a year & ten months. They are confined in Jail at Upper Marlborough Prince George's County Maryland.

> Grandison Briscoe, fugitive slave,
> on the fate of his wife who was recaptured

Dearest you told me you take few prisoners. May I say a little word, may I say, be merciful. Not that I do not think you so. But dearest as you say it is terrible to shoot a man begging for life on bended knees.

> Lizzie Little,
> to Union soldier George Avery, September 7, 1862

I'd think that the most forlorn picture of humanity is a Rebel Soldier taken prisoner on a very wet day.

> Allen Landis, Union soldier,
> letter to his parents, September 27, 1862

They gave me more coffee and ham than Jeff ever gave me.

> C. C. Brown, Confederate soldier,
> captured in Kentucky, December 9, 1862

It was never our intention that we should fight against the united States to Support a rotten government for Jeff Davis.

> Confederate prisoners of war,
> letter to their captors, October 6, 1863

The officers are all perfectly willing to stay and suffer here, so long as the public good may require, but desire very earnestly that Rebel officers may be placed in precisely our situation. We have no fires to warm us.

> Neal Dow, Union general, prisoner of war in Richmond,
> letter to Abraham Lincoln, November 12, 1863

The supply of wood issued to the prisoners during the winter was not enough to keep up the most moderate fires for two hours out of the twenty-four, and the only way to avoid freezing, was by unremitting devotion to the blankets . . . For my part, I never saw any one get enough of any thing to eat at Point Lookout, except the soup, and a tea spoonful of that was too much for ordinary digestion.

> Anthony Keiley, Confederate officer and prisoner of war
> at Point Lookout, Maryland, in 1864

There are deed, crimes, that may be forgiven; but this is not among them. It steeps its perpetrators in blackest, escapeless, endless damnation. Over fifty thousand have been compelled to die the death of starvation—reader, did you ever try to realize what starvation actually is?—in those prisons—and in a land of plenty!

> Walt Whitman, on the Southern military prisons

I am doing as well as you could expect for a prisoner . . . I pass a great portion of my time in reading the Holy Bible. I have read it through more than twice.

> Thee Jones, Confederate soldier from Kentucky,
> letter home from Camp Douglas, Chicago, December 1, 1864

"Thenceforward, and forever free": African Americans engage in their fight for equality

Emancipation Proclamation

Politics of Emancipation

Whipping and abuse are like laudanum: You have to double the dose as the sensibilities decline.

Harriet Beecher Stowe, *Uncle Tom's Cabin*

The courts are tribunals prescribed by the Constitution . . . Hence, whoever resists the final decision of the highest judicial tribunal arms a deadly blow at our whole republican system of government.

Stephen Douglas,
on the Supreme Court Dred Scott decision, 1846

You are loosened from your moorings, and are free; I am fast in my chains, and am a slave! You move merrily before the gentle gale, and I sadly before the bloody whip! You are freedom's swift-winged angels, that fly around the world; I am confined in bands of iron! O that I were free! O, that I were on one of the gallant decks, and under your protecting wing! Alas! betwixt me and you, the turbid waters flow. Go on, go on. O that I could also go! Could I but swim! If I could fly! O, why was I born a man, of whom to make a brute!

Frederick Douglass,
on watching ships sail the Chesapeake Bay

I was ordered to go for flowers, that my mistress's house might be decorated for an evening party. I spent the day gathering flowers and weaving them into festoons, while the dead body of my father was lying within a mile of me. What cared my owners for that? He was merely a piece of property. Moreover, they thought he had spoiled his children, by teaching them to feel that they were human beings. This was blasphemous doctrine for a slave to teach; presumptuous in him, and dangerous to the masters.

Harriet A. Jacobs,
Incidents in the Life of a Slave Girl, Written by Herself,
1861

Of all the Generals, high or low,
That help to save the nation,
There's none that strikes a harder blow
Than General Emancipation.

"The Old Union Wagon," a Union war song

Fire must be met with water, darkness with light, and war for the destruction of liberty, must be met with war for the destruction of slavery. The simple way, then, to put an end to the savage and desolating war now waged by the slaveholders, is to strike down slavery itself, the primal cause of that war.

Frederick Douglass, Douglass' Monthly, May 1861

May the point of our needles prick the slave owner's conscience.

Sarah Grimké, quilter

Sound policy, not less than humanity, demands the instant liberation of every slave in the rebel States.

Frederick Douglass, *Douglass' Monthly*, July 1861

If our Administration does not declare the Slaves Emancipated ere four weeks pass by I fear we are lost.

Lizzie Little,
letter to George Avery, Union soldier, January 12, 1862

The whites would tell their colored people not to go to the Yankees, for they would harness them to carts and make them pull the carts around, in place of horses. I asked grandmother, one day, if this was true. She replied, "Certainly not!" that the white people did not want the slaves to go over to the Yankees, and told them these things to frighten them.

Susie King Taylor, Savannah slave
who escaped in 1862, at age 14

God's ahead ob Massa Linkum. God won't let Massa Linkum beat de South till he do de right ting. Massa Linkum, he great man, and I'se poor nigger; but dis nigger can tell Massa Linkum how to save de money and de young men. He do it by setting de niggers free. S'pose dar was an awful big snake down dar, on de floor. He bite you. Folks all skeered, cause you die. You send for doctor to cut de bite; but the snake he rolled up dar, and while the doctor's dwine it, de snake he spring up and bite you agin, and so he keep dwine, till you kill him. Dat's what Massa Linkum orter know.

Harriet Tubman, quoted in a letter
from Lydia Maria Child, January 21, 1862

When President Lincoln declares the slaves emancipated I will declare myself no longer an American citizen.

George Avery, Union soldier,
letter to his future wife, January 26, 1862

When we cease to fight for the Union and begin to fight for Negro equality I am ready to lay down arms and will.

E.A.C. Taylor, Union soldier from Michigan, June 21, 1862

The Fight for Equality

I am quite sure there is not one man in ten but would feel himself degraded as a volunteer if negro equality is to be the order in the field of battle.

Writer for the *New York Times*, August 1862

To say we won't be soldiers because we cannot be colonels is like saying we won't go into the water till we have learned to swim.

Frederick Douglass,
responding to the Union's refusal to allow African American
soldiers to be officers *Douglass' Monthly*, March 1863

When the war trumpet sounded o'er the land, when men knew not the Friend from the Traitor, the Black man laid his life at the Altar of the Nation— and he was refused. When the arms of the Union were beaten, in the first year of the War, and the Executive called for more food for its ravaging maw, again the black man begged the privilege of aiding his Country in her need, to be again refused.

James Henry Gooding, 54th Massachusetts Volunteers,
letter to Abraham Lincoln, September 28, 1863

Now they want to cheat us out of what is justly due us, by paying us off with $10 per month, and taking three dollars out of that for clothing . . . Why are we not worth as much as white soldiers?

> Private in the 54th Massachusetts Volunteers, letter to his sister,
> quoted in the *Christian Recorder*, April 23, 1864

We came out to be true union soldiers the Grandsons of Mother Africa Never to Flinch from Duty.

> George Rodgers, Thomas Sipple, and Samuel Sampson,
> from camp in New Orleans, August 1864

Reactions to "The Day of Jubilee"

That on the first day of January, in the year of our Lord one thousand eight hundred and sixty-three, all persons held as slaves with any State or designated part of a State, the people whereof shall then be in rebellion against the United States, shall be then, thenceforward, and forever free.

> Abraham Lincoln,
> Emancipation Proclamation, September 22, 1862

God bless you for a good deed!

> Theodore Tilton, abolitionist editor of the *Independent*,
> letter to Abraham Lincoln, September 24, 1862

There is not a True Patriot or Philanthropist in the Union that does not heartily approve your recent . . . proclamation, on the Subject of Slavery . . . Allow me to congratulate you upon an assured and enviable immortality, whatever may be the result of this magnanimous vindication of the character of the Country and the rights of Humanity.

> David Paul Brown, Philadelphia,
> letter to Abraham Lincoln, September 25, 1862

I desire to express my undissembled and sincere thanks for your Emancipation Proclamation. It will stand as the great act of the age. It will prove to be wise in Statesmanship as it is Patriotic. It will be enthusiastically approved and sustained and future generations will, as I do, say God bless you for this great and noble act.

Hannibal Hamlin, vice-president of the United States,
letter to Abraham Lincoln, September 25, 1862

It is six days old, and while commendation in newspapers and by distinguished individuals is all that a vain man could wish . . . we have fewer troops in the field at the end of six days than we had at the beginning—the attrition among the old outnumbering the addition by the new. The North responds to the proclamation sufficiently in breath; but breath alone kills no rebels.

Abraham Lincoln,
letter to Vice-President Hamlin, September 28, 1862

Lincoln seems to be in a state of desperation.

Southern Illustrated News,
"A Note on the Emancipation Proclamation,"
October 11, 1862

Oh! long enslaved millions, whose cries have so vexed the air and sky, suffer on a few more days in sorrow, the hour of your deliverance draws nigh!

Frederick Douglass, *Douglass' Monthly,* October 1862

In giving freedom to the slave, we assure freedom to the free—honorable alike in what we give, and what we preserve. We shall nobly save, or meanly lose, the last best, hope of earth. Other means may succeed; this could not fail. The way is plain, peaceful, generous, just—a way which, if followed, the world will forever applaud, and God must forever bless.

Abraham Lincoln,
annual message to Congress, December 1, 1862

Men of my blood! Shake off the contempt of your proud oppressors. Enough of shame and submission; the break is complete! Down with the craven behavior of bondage!

> *L'Union*, African American journal from New Orleans,
> urging readers to take advantage of their new rights,
> December 6, 1862

Onst the time was, dat I cried all night. What's de matter? What's de matter? Matter enough. De nex morning my child was to be sold, an she was sold, and I neber spec to see her no more till de day ob judgment. Now, no more dat! no more dat! no more dat! Wid my hands agin my breast I was gwine to my work, when de overseer used to whip me along. Now, no more dat! no more dat! no more dat! . . . We's free now, bress de Lord! Dey can't sell my wife and child any more, bress de Lord! No more dat! no more dat! no more dat now!

> Ex-slave, at a meeting to celebrate the issuance
> of the final Emancipation Proclamation, December 31, 1862

I break your bonds and masterships,
And I unchain the slave:
Free be his heart and hand henceforth
As wind and wandering wave.

> Ralph Waldo Emerson (1803–1882),
> "Boston Hymn" read in Music Hall, January 1, 1863

Seeing such a multitude of people in and around my church, I hurriedly went up to the office of the first paper in which the proclamation of freedom could be printed, known as the "Evening Star," and squeezed myself through the dense crowd that was waiting for the paper. The first sheet run off with the proclamation in it was grabbed for by three of us, but some active young man got possession of it and fled. The next sheet was grabbed for by several, and was torn into tatters. The third sheet from the press was grabbed for by several, but I succeeded in procuring so much of it as contained the proclamation, and off I went for life and death . . . When the people saw me coming with the paper in my hand they raised a shouting cheer that was almost deafening . . . Mr. Hinton, to whom I handed the paper, read it with great force and clearness. While he was reading, every kind of demonstration and gesticulation was going on. Men squealed, women fainted, dogs barked, white and colored people shook hands, songs were sung . . . Great processions of colored and white men marched to and fro and passed in front of the White House and congratulated President Lincoln on his proclamation. The President came to the window and made responsive bows, and thousands told him, if he would come out of that palace, they would hug him to death. Mr. Lincoln, however, kept at a safe distance from the multitude, who were frenzied to distraction over his proclamation . . . It was indeed a time of times, and a half time, nothing like it will ever be seen again in this life.

Henry M. Turner, African American pastor,
remembering January 1, 1863, fifty years later

When I had crossed that line, I looked at my hands to see if I was the same person. There was such a glory over everything.

Harriet Tubman,
recalling her first escape from slavery, 1849

The President only makes provision for the emancipation of a part of an injured race . . . We believe those who are not immediately liberated will be ultimately benefited by this act, and that Congress will do something for those poor souls who will still remain in degradation.

Christian Recorder, African American weekly,
Philadelphia, January 3, 1863

You have added glory to the sky and splendor to the sun, & there are but few men who have ever done that before, either by word or act.

Gertrude, Victor Gus., and Katie Bloede, children from Brooklyn,
letter to Abraham Lincoln, January 4, 1863

The proclamation invites servile insurrection as an element in this emancipation crusade—a means of warfare, the inhumanity and diabolism of which are without example in civilized warfare.

Resolution passed by the state of Illinois,
"The Emancipation Proclamation Denounced,"
January 7, 1863

It had all the moral grandeur of a bill of lading.

Richard Hofstadter, historian,
of the Emancipation Proclamation,
The American Political Tradition

That proclamation frees the slave but ignores the Negro.

Wendell Phillips, abolitionist

The negro emancipation has been accomplished—the unfortunates have been thrust blindfold upon the ills of a state of which they know nothing. They enter with confidence and pleasure—expecting that freedom from care which they have hitherto enjoyed together with an entire immunity from all work or all necessity for self-provision. But on the threshold of their new life disappointment awaits them.

Catherine Edmondston, North Carolina

Only 8 men in Co. K approve the policy and proclamation of Mr. Lincoln. Many are deserting.

Levi Ross, Union soldier,
86th Illinois, February 3, 1863

The easiest, perhaps the only, way to achieve an adequate consensus for emancipation was to make it ancillary to winning the war.

Charles Royster, *The Destructive War*

As far as i can see there is no other cause for this war but Slavery and the sooner it is done the better for us.

James T. Miller, Union soldier, February 6, 1863

Although the proclamation was not made as an act of philanthropy, or as a great deed of justice due to those suffering in bonds, but simply as a war measure, still in it we recognize the hand of God; and for it we are constrained to say, roll forward the day when the American soil shall no more be polluted with that crime against God, American slavery.

> Resolution from a meeting of African Americans
> in Harrisburg, Pennsylvania, published in
> the *Christian Recorder*, February 7, 1863

We dont care much witch wa it gose sense we found ourt we are fitine for nigers.

> James R. French, Union soldier, April 2, 1863

The prejudice which repels the Negroes seems to increase in proportion as they are emancipated, and inequality is sanctioned by the manners while it is effaced from the laws of the country.

> Alexis de Tocqueville,
> French aristocrat who visited the United States in 1831

The conduct of the negroes, after the entrance of their "liberators," was beyond all expression. While the Yankee army was marching through the streets, crowds of them congregated on the sidewalks, with a broad grin of satisfaction on their ebony countenances . . . So arrogant did the negroes become after the entrance of the Federal forces, that no white Confederate citizen or soldier dared to speak to them.

> Alexander St. Clair Abrams, ex-Confederate soldier
> and reporter, on the fall of Vicksburg, Summer 1863

An entire race of mankind, yoked by selfishness to the collar of Slavery, is, by You, at the price of the noblest blood in America, restored to the dignity of Manhood, to civilization, and to Love . . . Greeting to you Abraham Lincoln great pilot of freedom; greeting to all who for two years have fought and bled around your regenerating Standard,—greeting to you, the redeemed offspring of Ham. The free men of Italy welcome the glorious rupture of your chains.

> G., M., and N. Garibaldi, Italian nationalists,
> letter to Abraham Lincoln, August 6, 1863

"What shall be done with the slaves if they are freed?" You had better ask, "What shall we do with the slaveholders if the slaves are freed?" The slave has shown himself better fitted to take care of himself than the slaveholder.

> William W. Brown, ex-slave, lecturer, and author, 1863

He took the opportunity to ask the [rebel] officers in a body what effect the President's Proclamation had produced in the South. Their reply was . . . that "it had played hell with them." Mr. Dean then asked them how that could be possible, since the negroes cannot read. To which one of them replied that one of his negroes had told him of the proclamation five days before he heard it in any other way.

> Peter Cooper, reporting an exchange
> between the provost-marshal of St. Louis and some
> Confederate officers in his charge, September 1863

His Emancipation proclamation is nothing more nor less than a premium for murdering men and outraging women. It is the most odious and atrocious outburst of brutal and cowardly vindictiveness that ever emanated from a pagan or "christian" tyrant.

> The Belfast News Letter, quoted in Camp and Field
> by Reverend Joseph Cross, Confederate army chaplain, 1864

I was keap in Slavy untell last Novr 1863. then the Good lord sent the Cornel borne [William Birney?] Down their in Marland in worsester Co So as I have been recently freed I have but letle to live on but I am Striveing Dear Sir but what I want to know of you Sir is is it possible for me to go & take my Children from those men that keep them in Savery

> John Q. A. Dennis, freedman to U.S. secretary of war
> Edwin M. Stanton, July 26, 1864

I'd been yere seventy-three years, workin' for my master widout even a dime wages. I'd worked rain-wet sun dry. I'd worked wid my mouf full of dust, but would not stop to get a drink of water. I'd been whipped, an' starved, an' I was always prayin', "Oh! Lord, come an' delibber us!" . . . I'd prayed seventy-three years, an' now he' come an' we's all free.

Elderly slave on the Sea Islands,
recounted by Harriet Tubman in
Scenes from the Life of Harriet Tubman
by Sarah Bradford, 1869

Them folks [Yankee soldiers] stood round there all day. Killed hogs and cooked them. Killed cows and cooked them. Took all kinds of sugar and preserves and things like that . . . Ma got scared and went to bed. Directly the lieutenant come on down there and said, "Auntie, get up from there. We aint a-going to do you no hurt. We're after helping you. We are freeing you. Aunt Dinah, you can do as you please now. You're free." She was free!

Matilda Hatchett, ex-slave from Arkansas,
remembering emancipation, 1930s

Echos: Martin Luther King, Jr.

Mr. President, I'd like to see you stand in this room and sign a Second Emancipation Proclamation outlawing segregation, one hundred years after Lincoln's.

Martin Luther King, Jr., to John F. Kennedy,
in the Lincoln Room of the White House, 1961

I have a dream that one day on the red hills of Georgia the sons of former slaves and the sons of former slaveowners will be able to sit down together at the table of brotherhood.

Martin Luther King, Jr.,
Civil Rights March on Washington, August 28, 1963

Fivescore years ago, a great American, in whose symbolic shadow we stand today, signed the Emancipation Proclamation. This momentous decree came as a great beacon light of hope to millions of Negro slaves who had been seared in the flames of withering injustice. It came as a joyous daybreak to end the long night of their captivity.

But one hundred years later, the Negro is still not free; one hundred years later, the life of the Negro is still sadly crippled by the manacles of segregation and the chains of discrimination; one hundred years later, the Negro lives on a lonely island of poverty in the midst of a vast ocean of material prosperity; one hundred years later, the Negro is still languished in the corners of American society and finds himself in exile in his own land.

Martin Luther King, Jr., "I Have a Dream," August 28, 1963

In 1863 the Negro was told that he was free as a result of the Emancipation Proclamation signed by Abraham Lincoln. But he was not given any land to make that freedom meaningful. It was something like keeping a person in prison for a number of years and suddenly discovering that that person is not guilty of the crime for which he was convicted. And you just go up to him and say, "Now you are free," but you don't give him any bus fare to get to town. You don't give him any money to get some clothes to put on his back or to get on his feet again in life. Every court of jurisprudence would rise up against this, and yet this is the very thing that our nation did to the black man.

Martin Luther King, Jr., March 31, 1968

Consecrating the battleground at Gettysburg, November 19, 1863

The Gettysburg Address

It is the desire that, after the Oration, You, as Chief Executive of the Nation, formally set apart these grounds to their Sacred use by a few appropriate remarks . . . it will kindle anew in the breasts of the comrades of these brave dead, who are now in the tented field or nobly meeting the foe in the front, a confidence that they who sleep in death on the Battle Field are not forgotten by those highest in authority; and they will feel that, should their fate be the same, their remains will not be uncared for.

David Wills, banker and Gettysburg civic leader,
letter inviting Abraham Lincoln to speak, November 2, 1863

Four score and seven years ago our fathers brought forth on this continent, a new nation, conceived in Liberty, and dedicated to the proposition that all men are created equal. Now we are engaged in a great civil war, testing whether that nation, or any nation so conceived and so dedicated, can long endure. We are met on a great battle-field of that war. We have come to dedicate a portion of that field, as a final resting place for those who here gave their lives that that nation might live. It is altogether fitting and proper that we should do this.

But, in a larger sense, we cannot dedicate—we cannot consecrate—we cannot hallow—this ground. The brave men, living and dead, who struggled here, have consecrated it, far above our poor power to add or detract. The world will little note, nor long remember what we say here, but it can never forget what they did here. It is for us the living, rather, to be dedicated here to the unfinished work which they who fought here have thus far so nobly advanced. It is rather for us to be here dedicated to the great task remaining before us—that from these honored dead we take increased devotion to that cause for which they gave the last full measure of devotion—that this nation, under God, shall have a new birth of freedom—and that this government of the people, by the people, for the people, shall not perish from the earth.

Abraham Lincoln, Gettysburg Address, November 19, 1863

Here let them rest together, they of the good cause and they of the evil . . . For neither was the one cause altogether good, nor the other altogether bad: the holier being clouded by much ignorance and selfishness, and the darker one brightened here and there with glorious flashes of self-devotion. It was not, rightly speaking, these brothers that were at war. The conflict was waged between two great principles—one looking towards liberty and human advancement, the other madly drawing the world back to barbarism and the dark ages. America was the chessboard upon which the stupendous game was played, and those we named Patriots and Rebels were but as the pawns.

John T. Trowbridge, Boston writer,
The South: A Tour of Its Battlefields and Ruined Cities,
A Journey Through the Desolated States,
and Talks with the People

The President, in a fine, free way, with more grace than is his wont, said his half dozen words of consecration.

John Hay, junior White House secretary,
diary entry, November 19, 1863

Something else [Lincoln] was as well—a literary craftsman—though so far this had gone unrecognized, unnoticed, and for the most part would remain so until critics across the Atlantic, unembarrassed by proximity, called attention to the fact . . . That there was such a thing as the American language, available for literary purposes, had scarcely begun to be suspected by the more genteel, except as it had been employed by writers of low dialog bits, which mainly served to emphasize its limitations. Lincoln's jogtrot prose, compacted of words and phrases still with the bark on, had no music their ears were attuned to; it crept by them.

Shelby Foote, *The Civil War*

Permit me also to express my great admiration of the thoughts offered by you, with such eloquent simplicity & appropriateness, at the consecration of the cemetery. I should be glad, if I came as near to the central idea of the occasion, in two hours, as you did in two minutes.

Edward Everett, scholar, diplomat, and principal
speaker at the dedication of Gettysburg, letter to
Abraham Lincoln, November 20, 1863

In our respective parts yesterday, you could not have been excused to make a short address, nor I a long one. I am pleased to know that, in your judgment, the little I did say was not entirely a failure.

Abraham Lincoln, reply to Edward Everett, November 20, 1863

The cheek of every American must tingle with shame as he reads the silly, flat and dishwatery utterances of the man who has to be pointed out to intelligent foreigners as the President of the United States.

Chicago *Tribune*,
report on Lincoln's address at Gettysburg, November 20, 1863

I think there is little chance of a happy hereafter for President Lincoln.

Kate Stone, Louisiana

[He is] the only earthly Pilot [who can be trusted to guide blacks to] Liberty and Equal Political rights.

> Chauncey Leonard, African American
> hospital chaplain, on Lincoln

It was to uphold this constitution, and the Union created by it, that our officers and soldiers gave their lives at Gettysburg. How dare he, then, standing on their graves, misstate the cause for which they died, and libel the statesmen who founded the government? They were men possessing too much self-respect to declare that negroes were their equals, or were entitled to equal privileges.

> Chicago *Sun Times,*
> "The President at Gettysburg," November 23, 1863

Echoes

By his words, he gave the field of battle a significance that it had lacked. For us and our country, he left Jefferson's ideals of freedom and equality joined to our Christian sacrificial act of death and rebirth. I believe this is a meaning that goes beyond sect or religion and beyond peace and war, and is now part of our lives as a challenge, obstacle, and hope.

> Robert Lowell, poet, at a tribute marking
> the centennial of the Gettysburg Address, 1963

They cannot be read, even, without kindling emotion.

> *Harper's Weekly,* of the words in the Gettysburg Address

Union field batteries

Sherman's March

If the people raise a howl against my barbarity and cruelty, I will answer that war is war, and not popularity seeking.

William T. Sherman, Union general,
recalling his words on entering Atlanta,
September 2, 1864, in his *Memoirs*, 1875

Then, presently, more soldiers came by, and this ended the passing of Sherman's army by my place, leaving me poorer by thirty thousand dollars than I was yesterday morning. And a much stronger Rebel!

Dolly Burge, Georgia

The Atlanta Hotel, Washington Hall, and all the square around the railroad depot, were soon in one sheet of flame. Drug stores, dry good stores, hotels, negro marts, theatres, and grog-shops were all now feeding the fiery element. Worn-out wagons and camp equipage were piled up in the depot and added to the fury of the flames . . .

The streets were now in one fierce sheet of flame; houses were falling on all sides, and fiery flakes of cinders were whirled about. Occasionally, shells exploded and excited men rushed through the choking atmosphere, and hurried away from the city of ruins.

David P. Conyngham, correspondent to the *New York Herald*,
on the burning of Atlanta, September 2, 1864

I did not much pity her. She was a regular secesh and spit out her spite and venom against the dirty Yanks and mudsills of the North.

Union soldier under General Sherman,
of a woman in Madison, Georgia

The white people came out of their houses to behold the sight, spite of their deep hatred of the invaders, and the Negroes were simply frantic with joy. Whenever they heard my name, they clustered about my horse, shouted and prayed in their peculiar style, which had a natural eloquence that would have moved a stone.

William T. Sherman, Union general,
remembering his 1864 March to the Sea

There has been no such army since the days of Julius Caesar.

Joseph Johnston, Confederate general,
on Sherman's invading troops

They [the Union soldiers] said that they didn't believe what I had belonged to me & I told them that I would swear that it belonged to me. I had tried to hide things. They found our meat, it was hid under the house & they took a crop of rice. They took it out & I had some cloth under the house too & the

dishes & two fine bed-quilts. They took them out . . . It didn't look like a
Yankee person would be so mean. But they said if they didn't take them the
whites here would & they [the whites] did take some of my things from their
camps after they [the Union soldiers] left.

Nancy Johnson, freedwoman, Georgia

Crowds of soldiers were tramping over the road in both directions; it was
like traveling through the streets of a populous town all day. They were
mostly on foot, and I saw numbers seated on the roadside greedily eating raw
turnips, meat skins, parched corn—anything they could find, even picking up
the loose grains that Sherman's horses had left.

Eliza Andrews, Georgia girl,
on Confederate soldiers retreating
in Sherman's wake, December 4, 1864

The cruelties practiced on this campaign towards citizens have been enough
to blast a more sacred cause than ours. We hardly deserve success.

Union corporal, writing from Savannah, 1864

I beg to present you as a Christmas gift the city of Savannah, with one hundred and fifty heavy guns and plenty of ammunition; also about twenty-five
thousand bales of cotton.

William T. Sherman, Union general,
wire to Abraham Lincoln, December 22, 1864

Many, many thanks for your Christmas-gift—the capture of Savannah . . .
Not only does it afford the obvious and immediate military advantages; but, in
showing to the world that your army could be divided, putting the stronger
part to an important new service, and yet leaving enough to vanquish the old
opposing force of the whole—Hood's army—it brings those who sat in darkness, to see a great light.

Abraham Lincoln,
letter to General Sherman, December 26, 1864

If Sherman has really left his army in the air and started off without a base to march from Georgia to South Carolina, he has done either one of the most brilliant or one of the most foolish things ever performed by a military leader.

Army and Navy Gazette, a British publication, 1864

Whatever he does, he will find no white faced women to do his bidding or ask his mercy, our choice would be death rather than dishonor.

Grace Elmore, South Carolina,
on the approach of General Sherman, December 31, 1864

Hail Columbia, happy land;
If we don't burn you, I'll be damned.

Marching song sung by the 15th Corps
on the way to Columbia, South Carolina

Can you imagine what it is like to ride all day in a wagon, no rest, no comfort, day after day, no chance to take a bath or even a wash, to beg for a tin basin of water too wash your children's faces and your own before going to sleep at night . . . with a baby in your arms, with scarcely nothing to feed her—breast milk dried up for want of nourishment—crying herself to sleep, hungry and sick, if it had rained all day no place to lay your blanket but in the wet and mud—to hush your little ones to sleep and roll them away from the cold and wind.

Harriette Keatinge, fleeing Columbia, South Carolina,
with Confederate troops, February 1865

Suddenly we heard the first gun, and for the first time heard the shriek of a shell pass overhead. It is hard to describe the stunned, giddy, confused realization that we were really being shelled—we helpless women and children!

Louis McCord, Columbia, South Carolina

Damn you women, you are the ones keeping up the war.

Union soldier, to the wife of the mayor of Columbia,
South Carolina, as she watched her house burn

Hundreds of iron safes, warranted "impenetrable to fire and the burglar," it was soon satisfactorily demonstrated, were not "Yankee proof."

> William Gilmore Simms, on the burning of Columbia,
> South Carolina, February 1865

Such a scene as this with the drunken, fiendish soldiery in their dark uniforms, infuriated, cursing, screaming, exulting in their work, came nearer realizing the material ideal of hell than anything I ever expect to see again. They call themselves "Sherman's Hellhounds."

> Emma LeConte, South Carolina,
> on the burning and pillage of Columbia, February 1865

With a base line of communication of 500 miles in Sherman's rear, through our own country, not a bridge has been burnt, a cart thrown from its track, nor a man shot by our people whose country has been desolated!

> Zebulon Vance, South Carolina governor,
> on the dearth of guerrilla interference
> with Sherman's March, 1865

I hope we may be able to exterminate the whole breed of Carolina, she is too overbearing and should be wiped out from the earth.

> Soldier in Sherman's army

Humiliation spreads her ashes over our homes and garments.

> William Gilmore Simms,
> on the burning of Columbia, South Carolina, February 1865

I took a little bird in its cage, which I could not bear to leave to the flames, in one hand, and my little child's hand in the other, and walked out from under our burning roof into the cold and pitiless street.

> Resident of Columbia, South Carolina,
> on the burning of her home, February 1865

The day has truly been so full of prosaic drudgery that there is no time for heroics.

Grace Elmore, South Carolina, after spending a day
hiding food from the approaching Union army

Carolina may dread us, she brought on the war and shall pay the penalty.

Soldier in Sherman's army, February 1865

Right in the line of breastworks stood a lone house. When we passed the house it was occupied only by women, not a single living man. They were surrounded by the bones of thousands of dead men.

Robert Strong, Union soldier under General Sherman,
on passing through the southeastern battlefields
on the march home, 1865

Part III. Aftermath of the War

⋆ ⋆ ⋆

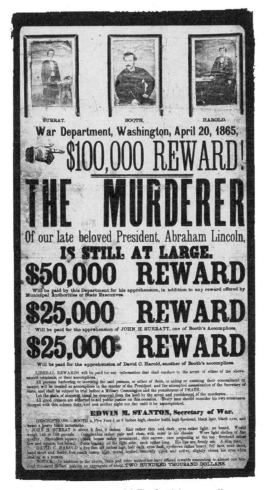

Sic semper tyrannis! *The South is avenged!*

Robert E. Lee surrenders to Ulysses S. Grant, McLean House, Appomattox

The War Ends

Surrender at Appomattox

Any proposition which embraces the restoration of peace, the integrity of the whole Union, and the abandonment of slavery, and which comes by and with an authority that can control the armies not at war against the United States will be received and considered by the Executive government of the United States, and will be met by liberal terms on other substantial and collateral points; and the bearer, or bearers thereof shall have safe-conduct both ways.

Abraham Lincoln,
letter "To Whom it May Concern," July 18, 1864

The President answered that . . . the offer was, in effect, a proposal that the Confederate States should surrender at discretion, admit that they had been wrong from the beginning of the contest, submit to the mercy of their enemies, and avow themselves to be in need of pardon for crimes; that extermination was preferable to such dishonor.

Judah P. Benjamin, Confederate secretary of state,
describing President Jefferson Davis's response to Union
terms of surrender, August 25, 1864

As to peace, I have said before, and now repeat, that three things are indispensable.

1. The restoration of the national authority throughout all the States.

2. No receding by the Executive of the United States on the slavery question . . .

3. No cessation of hostilities short of an end of the war, and the disbanding of all forces hostile to the government.

Abraham Lincoln, letter to John Campbell, April 5, 1865

How easily I could be rid of this, and be at rest. I have only to ride along the line and all will be over!

Robert E. Lee, Confederate general,
observing the encircling Union lines,
shortly before the surrender at Appomattox, April 9, 1865

What General Lee's feelings were I do not know. As he was a man of much dignity, with an impassable face, it was impossible to say whether he felt inwardly glad that the end had finally come, or felt sad over the result, and was too manly to show it.

Ulysses S. Grant, Union general, on the Confederate
surrender at Appomattox, April 9, 1865

I have probably to be General Grant's prisoner and thought I must make my best appearance.

Robert E. Lee, Confederate general,
explaining why he dressed in a new uniform
before the surrender at Appomattox, April 9, 1865

When news of the surrender first reached our lines, our men commenced firing a salute of a hundred guns in honor of the victory. I at once sent word, however, to have it stopped. The Confederates were now our prisoners, and we did not want to exult over their downfall.

> Ulysses S. Grant, Union general, on the Confederate
> surrender at Appomattox, April 9, 1865

After four years of arduous service marked by unsurpassed courage and fortitude, the Army of Northern Virginia has been compelled to yield to overwhelming numbers and resources. I need not tell the brave survivors of so many hard fought battles, who have remained steadfast to the last, that I have consented to this result from no distrust of them; but, feeling that valor and devotion could accomplish nothing that could compensate for the loss that must have attended the continuance of the contest, I have determined to avoid the useless sacrifice of those whose past services have endeared them to their countrymen.

> Robert E. Lee, Confederate general, General Orders No. 9,
> final order to the Army of Northern Virginia,
> April 10, 1865

I confess that I was fairly frightened at my own feelings as I saw the Army of Lee with its gray headed leader drawn up for surrender to us as their conquerors. The awful magnitude of the crisis, the remembrance of the weeping and wailing, and treasure and blood their crimes has cost were all sunk in a spirit of forgiveness and of mercy and had it been left to me I much fear that then and there I should have restored to full citizenship every man from Gen. Lee down.

> George Anthony, Union captain, April 21, 1865

Conquered

Again and again we shall return, until the baffled and exhausted enemy shall abandon in despair his endless and impossible task of making slaves of a people resolved to be free.

> Jefferson Davis, Confederate president,
> when the Confederate government
> fled Richmond, one week before Lee's surrender
> at Appomattox, April 1865

Let us suffer still more, give up yet more—anything, anything that will help the cause, anything that will give us freedom and not force us to live with such people—to be ruled by such horrible and contemptible creatures—to submit to them when we hate them so bitterly.

Emma LeConte, South Carolina, 1865

To submit to our enemies now, would be more infamous than it would have been in the beginning. It would be cowardly yielding to power what was denied upon principle. It would be to yield the cherished right of self-government, and to acknowledge ourselves wrong in the assertion of it; to brand the names of our slaughtered companions as traitors; to forfeit the glory already won; to lose the fruits of all the sacrifices made and the privations gained, and bring certain ruin, disgrace, and eternal slavery upon our country . . . Is life so dear, or peace so sweet, as to be purchased at the price of chains and slavery? Forbid it Heaven!

McGowan's Brigade, South Carolina volunteers,
resolutions against surrender, 1865

Excitement among the officers and men is intense. Many propose to fight out to the bitter end, rather than to surrender.

John Paris, Confederate army chaplain,
North Carolina regiment, April 9, 1865

Could the report be true? . . . Was not Lee still there? Were his soldiers not as brave, as heroic as ever? No, the report of a surrender at Appomattox was merely another vile Yankee invention!

Elizabeth Avery Meriwether, Alabama

I was so completely stunned by the thought that all the suffering, all the spilt blood, all the poverty, all the desolation of the South was for naught; that her very fidelity, heroism, and fortitude, qualities so noble in themselves, had wrought her undoing, that I seemed to become dead to everything around me. . . . Insensibility at a crucial moment may be nature's anaesthesia.

Mrs. Roger Pryor, on learning of the surrender at Appomattox

General Lee is not the Confederacy.

> Mrs. Robert E. Lee, on the surrender at Appomattox

I shuddered at the dreadful silence. Richmond burning and no alarm.

> Mary Burrows Fontaine, Virginia, April 30, 1865

Nothing can be more amusing than the efforts of some of the most violent rebels, who in other days never let an opportunity pass to show their love for Jeff Davis, or manifest their vindictive feelings against the negroes in every conceivable manner, to cultivate the friendship of the colored people, with the hope that the forgiving nature of the race may induce them to forget the wrongs of the past.

> T. Morris Chester, African American correspondent
> to the *Philadelphia Press*, on entering Richmond
> soon after the evacuation of the Confederates, April 1865

It is marvelous that a people that a month ago had money, armies, and the attributes of a nation should today be no more, and that we live, breathe, move, talk as before—will it be so when the soul leaves the body behind it?

> Josiah Gorgas,
> Confederate general and chief of ordnance, May 4, 1865

We are scattered, demoralized, stunned—ruined.

> Mary Chesnut, May 15, 1865

I am for Virginia going down to history, proudly and starkly, with the title of a subjugated people . . . rather than as a people who ever submitted, and bartered their honour for the mercy of an enemy.

> Edward A. Pollard, Confederate editor,
> "A Letter on the State of the War," 1865

The war is over, and we are a Subjugated people, perfectly right, just as it should be, we are too damned worthless and corrupt to be in any other condition.

William Morris, Confederate surgeon, June 1865

Conqueror

Surrender of Lee's army, ten cents and no mistake.

Cry of the newspaper boy in New York City, April 10, 1865

The people poured into the streets, frenzied with gladness, until there seemed to be no men and women in Chicago—only crazy, grown-up boys and girls.

Mary Livermore,
describing how news of Lee's surrender was received

I am sorry the war is ended. Pray do not think me murderous. No; but all the punishment we could inflict on the rebels would not atone for one drop of blood so cruelly spilled. I would exterminate them root and branch. They have often said they preferred it before subjugation, and with the help of God, I would give it them.

T. R. Keenan, Union soldier,
after Lincoln's assassination, April 1865

One hundred thousand dollars reward in gold, will be paid to any person who will apprehend and deliver Jefferson Davis to any of the military authorities.

Order issued by J. H. Wilson, Union general,
four days before Davis was captured, May 6, 1865

Better years of battle than a peace like this is the cry of all we see.

Kate Stone, Louisiana, May 20, 1865

By your patriotic devotion to your country in the hour of danger and alarm, your magnificent fighting, bravery, and endurance, you have maintained the supremacy of the Union and the Constitution, overthrown all armed opposition to the enforcement of the laws and of the proclamation forever abolishing Slavery—the cause and pretext of the Rebellion—and opened the way to the rightful authorities to restore order and inaugurate peace on a permanent and enduring basis on every foot of American soil . . . Victory has crowned your patriotic hearts; and, with the gratitude of your countrymen and the highest honor a great and free nation can accord, you will soon be permitted to return to your homes and families, conscious of having discharged the highest duty of American citizens.

> Ulysses S. Grant, Union general,
> message to the Union army, June 2, 1865

There never was a beardless country boy any prouder than I was at the age of 22 years as I marched up thru the city of Washington and went past the reviewing stand.

> Frank L. Ferguson, Union captain,
> on the grand review of Union troops

What matters the loss of all these years? What matters the trial, the sickness, the wounds! What we went out to do is done. The war is ended, and the Union is saved!

> Ted Upson, Union soldier from Indiana

The death of Abraham Lincoln, April 15, 1865

The Assassination

✯ ✯ ✯

He [President Abraham Lincoln] has a face like a hoosier Michael Angelo, so awful ugly it becomes beautiful, with its strange mouth, its deep-cut, criss-cross lines, and its doughnut complexion.

Walt Whitman, letter, March 19, 1863

Unquestionably, Western man though he be, and Kentuckian by birth, President Lincoln is the essential representative of all Yankees, and the veritable specimen, physically, of what the world seems determined to regard as our characteristic qualities.

Nathaniel Hawthorne

Lincoln was fond of the theatre. I have myself seen him there several times. I remember thinking how funny it was that he, in some respects the leading actor in the stormiest drama known to real history's stage through the centuries, should sit there and be so completely interested in those human jackstraws, moving about with their silly little gestures, foreign spirit, and flatulent text.

Walt Whitman, 1890

J. Wilkes Booth he moves down the aisle,
He had measured once before,
He passes Lincoln's bodyguard
A-nodding at the door.

He holds a dagger in his right hand,
A pistol in his left,
He shoots poor Lincoln in the temple,
And sends his soul to rest.

"Booth Killed Lincoln," folk song

Sic semper tyrannis!
(The South is avenged!)

John Wilkes Booth,
after shooting Abraham Lincoln, April 14, 1865

I went to the theatre and there I seen the President shot . . . There was the greatest time cheering and shouting when he came in but there was no such a time when he went out.

Gertrude Dunn, April 14, 1865

Four years ago, O Illinois, we took from your midst an untried man . . . we return him to you a mighty conqueror. Not thine any more, but the Nation's; not ours, but the world's. Give him place, ye prairies.

Henry Ward Beecher, Brooklyn preacher,
sermon in anticipation of Lincoln's
funeral procession, April 1865

Now he belongs to the ages.

Edwin M. Stanton, U.S. secretary of war,
at Lincoln's death, April 15, 1865

When I think of the death of our President, it seems as if it was my own flesh and blood that had been called away.

Union soldier's wife

Humanity has lost a firm advocate, our race its Patron Saint, and the good of all the world a fitting object to emulate . . . The name Abraham Lincoln will ever be cherished in our hearts, and none will more delight to lisp his name in reverence than future generations of our people.

Edgar Dinsmore, African American soldier from New York,
on Lincoln's assassination, in a letter to his fiancée

I must say, and I am proud to say, that I never was treated by any one with more kindness and cordiality than were shown to me by that great and good man, Abraham Lincoln . . . He took my little book, and with the same hand that signed the death-warrant of slavery, he wrote as follows: "For Aunty Sojourner Truth, Oct. 29, 1864. A. Lincoln."

Sojourner Truth, reflecting on her October 29, 1864,
meeting with Lincoln

The colored people have lost their best friend on earth; Mr. Lincoln was our best friend, and I will give five dollars of my wages towards erecting a monument to his memory.

Charlotte Scott of Virginia, freed slave,
to her former mistress, Mrs. William P. Rucker

None but cowardly, treacherous nations ever resort to such means to rid themselves of an enemy.

> Annie Harper, a Southerner, on Lincoln's assassination

God saw this as necessary in finishing up this great rebellion. He saw that the good and kind-hearted man would not be the one for this work; for he has taken him away.

> E. E. Adams,
> in the *Philadelphia Evening Bulletin,* April 17, 1865

The rebs won't let us alone. If they can't kill us, they'll kill all our frien's, sure.

> Jack Flowers, ex-slave from South Carolina,
> on Lincoln's assassination

We greeted his death in a spirit of reckless hate, and hailed it as bringing agony and bitterness to those who were the cause of our agony and bitterness. To us Lincoln was an inhuman monster.

> John S. Wise, Virginia, on the South's reaction
> to Lincoln's assassination, *The End of an Era,* 1899

All honor to J. Wilkes Booth, who has rid the world of a tyrant and made himself famous for generations . . . How earnestly we hope our [avenger] may escape to the South, where [he] will [be met] with a warm welcome.

> Kate Stone, Louisiana

We have suffered till we feel savage.

> Emma LeConte, South Carolina,
> on why Southerners were thrilled
> to hear of Lincoln's assassination

My only fear now is that the war will end and we have no opportunity to avenge his death upon the vile traitors.

Christopher Keller, Union lieutenant,
on Lincoln's assassination

They have slain Mercy and now they must abide by the sterner master, Justice.

John F. Brobst, Union soldier from Wisconsin,
on the South after Lincoln's assassination

Echoes

Caesar had his Brutus! Charles the First his Cromwell, and Abraham Lincoln his John Wilkes Booth!

Thomas N. Norwood, Georgian lawyer,
A Vindication of the South, 1917

He was a sad, lost man chanting a rhythm of the sad and lost.

Carl Sandburg, poet and biographer,
on President Lincoln

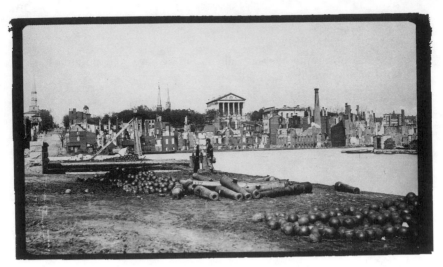

View from the south side of the canal basin, Richmond

Making Peace

As I look back to Bull Run, Fort Donelson, the Seven Days, Antietam, Gettysburg, Chancellorsville, and other battles, I wonder my thoughts have not been more engrossed by the developments of the great tragedy, that I have been able to pay any attention to my common routine and to be interested in anything outside the tremendous chapter that history has been taking down in shorthand.

George T. Strong, 1861

So it came to pass that as he trudged from the place of blood and wrath that his soul changed. He came from hot plowshares to prospects of clover tranquilly, and it was as if hot plowshares were not. Scars faded as flowers. It rained.

Stephen Crane, *The Red Badge of Courage*

I am for a tidal wave of peace—and I am not alone.

> Wife of a Confederate officer, letter to Mrs. Roger A. Pryor

Our policy is, as you say, peace, it is our sentiment also.

> Jefferson Davis, Confederate president, confidential letter to
> Supreme Court justice and intermediary for the Confederacy,
> John Campbell, April 6, 1861

With malice toward none; with charity for all; with firmness in the right, as God gives us to see the right, let us strive on to finish the work we are in; to bind up the nation's wounds; to care for him who shall have borne the battle, and for his widow, and his orphan—to do all which may achieve and cherish a just, and a lasting peace, among ourselves, and with all nations.

> Abraham Lincoln, second Inaugural Address, March 4, 1865

I have too exalted an opinion of the American people to believe that they will consent to injustice; and it is only necessary, in my opinion, that truth should be known, for the rights of every one to be secured. I know of no surer way of eliciting the truth than by burying contention with the war.

> Robert E. Lee, Confederate general, September 7, 1865

The dead are dead—let that atone:
And though with equal hand we strew
The blooms on saint and sinner too,
Yet God will know to choose his own.

> Ambrose Bierce (1842–1914), "To E. S. Salomon,"
> who in a Memorial Day oration protested bitterly
> against decorating the graves of Confederate dead

The past is dead; let it bury its dead, its hopes, and its aspirations. Before you lies the future, a future full of golden promise, a future of expanding national glory, before which all the world shall stand amazed. Let me beseech you to lay aside all rancor, all bitter sectional feeling, and to take your places in the ranks of those who will bring about a consummation devoutly to be wished— a reunited country.

Jefferson Davis, Confederate president,
from his final speech, delivered to a convention
of young Southerners

Now that the battle rage is over,
Now that the minute guns are cold,
Oh haste, knit again,
What the sword has cleft in twain,
Be friends and brothers, as of old.

Post war song

As one of the disfranchised race, I would say to every colored soldier, "Bring your gun home."

African American soldier,
on the precariousness of peace between
blacks and whites in Louisiana, after racial violence
upon the return of delegates from the 1865 black conventions

It is worse than all to see the change that is taking place, it may be right but it is hard to see men quietly, cheerfully falling into the new state of things, taking the oath, going into office, talking of the President and of the Government as if there had never been Our President Davis and our government.

Sarah Wadley, September 26, 1865

We elms of Malvern Hill
Remember every thing;
But sap the twig will fill:
Wag the world how it will,
Leaves must be green in Spring.

Herman Melville (1819–1891), "Malvern Hill"

The women of Columbus, Mississippi, animated by nobler sentiments than many of their sisters, have shown themselves impartial in their offerings made to the memory of the dead. They strewed flowers alike on the graves of the Confederate and of the National Soldiers.

New York Tribune, news item, 1867

They feel no gratitude towards us and I feel no obligations to them.

Howell Cobb, former slaveowner,
on relations with his former slaves

The former relations has to be unlearnt by both parties.

Southern planter, on making peace after the end of slavery

Let us have peace.

Ulysses S. Grant, campaign slogan,
1868 presidential elections

Irrational prejudices and passions are gradually giving way to reason and an enlightened conservatism.

Mississippi Educational Journal, regarding the local
attitude toward biracial schools, April 1871

Nor even in the dying hour / While passing calm away / Can we forget or e'er regret / The wearin' of the gray!

Postbellum South

Aftermath

It is a common, an every-day sight in Randolph county, that of women and children, most of whom were formerly in good circumstances, begging for bread from door to door.

Accounts of the Freedmen's Bureau in Alabama, 1865

Now we are a subjugated People . . . How did it befall us, that is [the] worst part. We conquored ourselves, comitted Suicide—such a people does not deserve independance.

J. W. Yale, May 1865

Everybody or almost everybody seems to be trying to forget the war & the past four years of agony & bloodshed, but I never can & rather cherish every memory connected with it.

Emma Homes, Charleston, 1865

There has probably never been a people, since the Gauls, so thoroughly beaten in war as the Southerners have been. The completeness of their overthrow has been in the exact ration of the vigor and obstinacy of their resistance, and resistance more vigorous and more obstinate was probably never offered by any population of the same size.

E. L. Godkin, editorial in the *Nation,* September 21, 1865

Seldom has there been a more hopeless chaos out of which to construct a new order of things than Charleston presented in those days. Yet the process of amelioration has year by year been steadily going forward.

Robert Summers, *Southern States,* 1870

We are waning, in prosperity every year, & unless some beneficial change can be effected our ruin, utter & total, is only a question of time. Fences & houses are falling into decay & our old lands are constantly depreciating in value.

Herschel V. Johnson, November 12, 1872

The South & West are wretchedly poor and are growing poorer every day.

L. Q. Washington, February 11, 1874

Everything went into Confederate securities; everything to eat and everything to wear was consumed, and when the war suddenly ended there was nothing left but absolute poverty and nakedness. Famine followed, and suffering beyond computation, the story of which has never been told.

J. S. Pike, *The Prostrate State*

Bitterness

No one can imagine the bitterness that exists between what were once called friends.

Sallie Pendleton Van Rensselaer,
on what would become West Virginia, January 13, 1862

Submission; submission! Why do I speak that disgraceful word, why do I think it for a moment; victory or death is our only alternative, worse than death would be our conquest by the Yankees.

Sarah Wadley, March 2, 1862

Teach my children to hate them with that bitter hatred that will never permit them to meet under any circumstances without seeking to destroy each other. I know the breach is now wide & deep between us & let it widen & deepen until all Yankees or no Yankees are to live in the South.

T. W. Montfort, Confederate soldier from Georgia,
letter to his wife, March 18, 1862

There were a number of Yankees buried in our graveyard. I think it outrageous to fill up our Cemetery with such trash.

Rachel Craighead, Nashville, Spring 1862

If there is any one in this wide world who hates the Yankee race worse than I do, I am sorry for him, because he must have devoted his whole heart to the work.

Howell Cobb, Georgia secessionist

Don't expect to overcome such a country or subdue such a people in one, two, or five years, it is the task of half a century.

William T. Sherman, Union general,
letter to his brother, August 1863

The traveller or visitor might observe a large number of daily rebel newspapers well sustained, while a single loyal paper is sustained with difficulty. He might discover that the rebel merchant or lawyer is full of business and growing rich, while the loyalist either fails, or is driven to pander and dissimulate. And he may find that the rebel chaplain preaches to overflowing houses, while the loyal minister is in truth a missionary in an unfriendly country.

Unionist statement,
Report of Joint Committee on Reconstruction, 1865

We know that we were Rebels,
We don't deny the name,
We speak of that which we have done
With grief, but not with shame!
And we never will acknowledge
That the blood the South has spilt
Was shed defending what we deemed
A cause of wrong and guilt.

Southern post war song

You cannot expect us to treat the northern people well who come here, or to have any intercourse with them. They have humiliated us, and we cannot buy, or sell, or have any intercourse with them.

Virginia woman, on Northerners, 1865

I hereby declare my unmitigated hatred to Yankee rule . . . and to the Yankee race . . . May such sentiments be held universally in the outraged and downtrodden South, although in silence & stillness, until the now far-distant day shall arrive for just retribution for Yankee usurpation, oppression, & atrocious outrages—& for deliverance and vengeance for the now ruined, subjugated & enslaved Southern States!

Edmund Ruffin, secessionist,
final entry in his diary before shooting himself, June 1865

You have no right to ask, or expect that she will at once profess unbounded love to that Union from which for four years she tried to escape at the cost of her best blood and all her treasure. Nor can you believe her to be so unutterably hypocritical, so base, as to declare that the flag of the Union has already usurped in her heart the place which has so long been sacred to the "Southern Cross."

Wade Hampton, letter to Andrew Johnson, 1866

The people who felt most bitterly at the end of the war were not the majority in numbers but they were the majority so to speak in social rank and influence, refinement, intelligence and wealth.

Cornelia Phillips Spencer, North Carolina

If I were made Governor, I would have the whole State in another war in less than a week.

Jubal Early, former Confederate general,
on a proposal that he run for governor
of Virginia, February 17, 1867

Racism

It is hard for the old slaveholding spirit to die. But die it must.

Sojourner Truth, abolitionist and former slave,
October 1, 1865

That child is already born who will behold the last negro in the State of Mississippi.

> The Natchez, Mississippi, *Democrat*,
> predicting that freed blacks wouldn't survive, 1865

The white folks had all the courts, all the guns, all the hounds, all the rail-roads . . . all the newspapers, all the money, and nearly all the land—and we had only our ignorance, our poverty and our empty hands.

> Freed slave and survivor of a Georgia forced-labor camp

There is nothing in this country for a black man that has common sense but cruelty, starvation and bloodshed.

> Charles Snyder,
> on the verge of emigrating to Liberia, February 1, 1868

A white man in a white man's place. A black man in a black man's place. Each according to the eternal fitness of things.

> Motto of the Forest, Mississippi, *Register*, 1875

The Southern Character

Moral justice dissents from the habitual sneer, denunciation, and malediction, which have become consecrated forms of piety in speaking of the South.

> Julia Ward Howe, 1858

I wish I was in the land of cotton,
Ole times there are not forgotten;
Look away, look away, look away, Dixie land.
In Dixie Land where I was born in,

Early on one frosty mornin',
Look away, look away, look away, Dixie land.

I wish I was in Dixie! Hooray! Hooray!
In Dixie Land, I'll take my stand,
To live and die in Dixie.
Away, away, away down south in Dixie.
Away, away, away down south in Dixie.

"Dixie," 1859

To speak of subjugating such a people, so united and determined, is to speak
a language incomprehensible to them.

Jefferson Davis, Confederate president,
on the Confederacy, to the Confederate Congress

Why has the South become so toadyish and sycophantic? I think it is
because the best and noblest were killed off during the war and that the scum
element is now in the ascendancy.

D. H. Hill, former Confederate general, after the war

Let us cling to our identity as a people! The danger is upon us of losing it—of
its being absorbed and swallowed up in that of a people which, having
despoiled us of the rights of freemen, assumes to do our thinking, our legislat-
ing, and our ruling for us . . . Nothing of the past will be left to the South but
a history which will read like an elegiac poem, nothing for the present but a
place of the maps which our children study.

Reverend John L. Giradeau, in Charleston's Magnolia
Cemetery, Confederate Memorial Day 1871

When Walker Percy won the National Book Award, newsmen asked him
why there were so many good Southern writers and he said, "Because we lost
the War." He didn't mean by that simply that a lost war makes good subject
matter. What he was saying was that we have had our Fall. We have gone into

the modern world with an inburnt knowledge of human limitations and with a sense of mystery which could not have developed in our first state of inno-cence—as it has not sufficiently developed in the rest of our country.

Flannery O'Connor, novelist,
"The Regional Writer," Georgia, 1962

The Southern passion for military service first astonished the rest of the coun-try in 1898, when Southerners signed up in droves to avenge the *Maine*. It was the country's first war since Appomattox, and for thirty-three years Yankees had questioned Southern loyalty. The intense patriotism of Southerners per-sists to this good day . . . "Has your boy done his service yet?" is a common question in the South.

Molly Ivins, *Molly Ivins Can't Say That, Can She?*

In the last third of the nineteenth century Southerners found it easy, or at least expedi-ent, to forget a great deal of what they had known about the Confederacy, to reshape its history, and to remember things that had not occurred.

Charles Royster, *The Destructive War*, 1991

Despite all the physical destruction and death that violence accomplished, the North failed to destroy the South spiritually.

Strom Thurmond, 1993

Echoes

The Southern men were too busy trying to retrieve their fallen fortunes, but the women—they had more time to brood over the wrongs that had been done them, they had not had the excitement of battle to sustain them, they suffered even more than their husbands and sons and brothers. For these rea-sons, or perhaps just because women are less forgiving than men, it took the women of the South a long time before they were able to feel kindly toward their conquerors. To this day I cannot truly say I love a Yankee.

Elizabeth Avery Meriwether,
more than 50 years after Appomattox

i am in the darkness of the south and i am trying to get out.

African American from Alabama,
letter to the *Chicago Defender*, 1917

What kills us here is that we jest can't make it 'cause they pay us nothing for what we give them, and they charge us double price when they sell it back to us.

Southern African American sharecropper, 1930s

May 17, 1954 may be recorded by future historians as a black day of tragedy for the South and for both races.

The Jackson, Mississippi, *Clarion Ledger*,
on the *Brown* v. *Board of Education* decision

Does the man who, in the relative safety of mob anonymity, stands howling vituperation at a little Negro girl being conducted into a school building, feel himself at one with those gaunt, barefoot, whiskery scarecrows who fought it out, breast to breast, to the death, at the Bloody Angle at Spotsylvania, in May 1864?

Robert Penn Warren, *The Legacy of the Civil War*

Slavery was not all that bad.

Frances Chapman, retired nurse in Todd County, Kentucky,
statement made on the radio, 1995

The Only Reason You Are White Today Is Because Your Ancestors Practiced
& Believed in Segregation YESTERDAY.

> Heading on a flier handed out by the Ku Klux Klan,
> Todd County, Kentucky, 1995

Trust me. The South is no place for beginners. Its power of denial can turn a
lost war into a vibrant, necessary form of national chic.

> Allan Gurganus, Southern author,
> in a *New York Times* opinion piece, December 8, 1996

American by Birth, Rebel by the Grace of God.

> T-shirt slogan

Follow west the paths of defeated Confederate soldiers and you find the roots
of Western suspicion of Washington . . . The crises and cultural clashes now
splitting us apart simply trace out the fault lines of our society laid down long
ago, along which it fractures in times of stress.

> Peter Marin, on the Freemen in Montana, December 1996

They say that war ended a long time ago. But around here it's like it's still
going on.

> Father of Michael Westerman, Todd County, Kentucky,
> teenager killed for flying a Confederate flag on his truck, 1996

In the south, the war is what A.D. is elsewhere: they date from it.

> Mark Twain, American writer

The ruins in Charleston

Reconstruction

Government and Politics

Neither slavery nor involuntary servitude, except as a punishment for crime whereof the party shall have been duly convicted, shall exist within the United States, or any place subject to their jurisdiction.

The Thirteenth Amendment to the Constitution,
December 18, 1865

If I were in your place, I'd let 'em up easy—let 'em up easy.

Abraham Lincoln, responding to
General Godfrey Weitzel's question about
how to treat the conquered people in his charge, 1865

The President has, in his efforts at the reconstruction of the civil government of the States, late in rebellion, left us entirely at the mercy of those subjugated but unconverted rebels in everything save the privilege of bringing us, our wives and little ones, to the auction block.

Petition of African American Virginians to Congress, 1865

No negro or freedman shall be permitted to rent or keep a house within the limits of the town under any circumstances. . . . No freedman shall sell, barter, or exchange any article of merchandise within the limits of Opelousas without the permission in writing from his employer.

Ordinance, Opelousas, Louisiana, 1865

When all the citizens of a state reach the point at which they are ready to return, upon the bases of government which the war has made for us all, let them return. But not until the institutions of these states conform to the highest civilization of the land.

George Loring, Massachusetts abolitionist, after the war

Much ill-feeling has been kept alive by the United States Treasury agents . . . They would propose to seize a man's property in the name of the United States, but abandon the claim on the payment of heavy bribes, which of course went into their own pockets.

J. T. Trowbridge, The South, 1865

This cotton business should be wound up and the entire lot of cotton agents withdrawn from the South. The subordinates under the principal agents are roving over the country and harassing the people without any corresponding benefit to the national treasury.

H. M. Watterson, agent of the president
for the investigation of cotton frauds in the South, 1866

If any white person and any negro, or the descendant of any negro, to the
third generation inclusive . . . intermarry, or live in adultery or fornication
with each other, each of them must, on conviction, be imprisoned in the peni-
tentiary, or sentenced to hard labor for the county, for not less than two, nor
more than seven years.

Penal Code of Alabama, 1866

The South has done more in fourteen months than I expected to see accomplished in several years. Slavery is abolished. The Confederate debt is repudi-
ated. The people are submissive. What more do you want? Why do you go on
demanding exaction after exaction?

U.S. President Andrew Johnson,
to a group of radical Republican congressmen, 1866

Said rebel States shall be divided into military districts and made subject to
the military authority of the United States.

First Reconstruction Act, vetoed by President Johnson,
and passed over the veto on the same day, March 2, 1867

The tendency is to ignore virtue and property and intelligence—and to put
the powers of government into the hands of mere numbers . . . The majority
in all times and in all countries are improvident and without property.
Agrarianism and anarchy must be the result of this ultra democracy.

Jonathan Worth, governor of North Carolina,
February 16, 1868

The peace to which Grant invites us is the peace of despotism and death.

Francis P. Blair Jr., Democratic candidate for
vice-president, on the Reconstruction laws, July 13, 1868

It is reconstruction and the issues growing out of it which preserve the unity of the Republican party. Strip them of the support which their question gives them and their dissolution will speedily follow.

E. G. Cabaniss, Georgia chairman of the Democratic party,
June 24, 1869

Whereas it is essential to just government we recognize the equality of all men before the law, and hold that it is the duty of government in its dealings with the people to mete out equal and exact justice to all, of whatever nativity, race, color, or persuasion, religious or political; and it being the appropriate object of legislation to enact great fundamental principles into law: Therefore, Be it enacted, That all persons within the jurisdiction of the United States shall be entitled to the full and equal enjoyment of the accommodations, advantages, facilities, and privileges of inns, public conveyances on land or water, theaters, and other places of public amusement; subject only to the conditions and limitations established by law, and applicable alike to citizens of every race and color, regardless of any previous condition of servitude.

The Civil Rights Act of 1875

The Present Constitution of Alabama was intended to make the negro the Political master of the white man. Let us frame a new one, which will do justice to the white counties.

Mobile *Register*, January 27, 1875

Shall the people of the states or the corrupt Federal officers rule in this and all the other states?

Zebulon B. Vance, former Confederate governor
and gubernatorial candidate, North Carolina, 1876

The Republicans just did not understand the stealing business, while they steal chickens, the Democrats steal millions of dollars.

Thomas Settle, Republican gubernatorial candidate,
North Carolina, 1876

Gloria in Excelsis, North Carolina is redeemed. The nation is saved.

The Raleigh *News*, on the victory of the Democratic candidate
for governor in 1876, signaling the end of Reconstruction

The Republican party was never indigenous to Southern soil. In truth, it has never become acclimated there, but has remained from the first an exotic.

Albion Tourgée, Union veteran,
carpetbagger, and writer, 1878

Northern Opinion

No position for the Negro that would satisfy the South would agree with enlightened opinion in the North. But how can the North enforce its views? Only by such an exertion of power of the general government as would be inconsistent with its plan & theory.

Sidney George Fisher, Pennsylvania, 1865

Can they be trusted with the sole management of one of the most difficult and delicate of political processes, the endowment of slaves with the feelings and aspirations of freemen, when they have up to the last moment fought against it sword in hand, and at this moment make no secret of the loathing and rage which it excites in them, of their confidence that it will fail, and of their hopes that it may fail?

E. L. Godkin, editorial in the *Nation*,
on the Southern states, September 21, 1865

No white man can live in the South in the future and act with any other than the Democratic party unless he is willing and prepared to live a life of social isolation and remain in political oblivion.

Mississippi "scalawag" (loyal Unionist), after the war

The practice of regarding everything left in the country as the legitimate prize to the first officer who discovers it, has led, in some cases, to performances little creditable to the national uniform. What shall be thought of the officer who, finding a fine law library, straightway packed it up and sent it to his office in the North?

Whitelaw Reid, *After the War,* 1865

The word expressed all that collective and accumulated hate which generations of antagonism had engendered, intensified and sublimated by the white-heat of a war of passionate intensity and undoubted righteousness to the hearts of its promoters.

Albion Tourgée, Union veteran and writer, on carpetbaggers

I came out with the kindest feelings for these people down here; I wanted to see it made easy; we had whipped them, and I wanted it to rest there. I thought the South wanted it to end there. But I was tremendously mistaken. They hate us and despise us and all belonging to us. They call us cut-throats, liars, thieves, vandals, cowards, and the very scum of the earth.

A carpetbagger quoted in the *Nation,* April 1866

The enemies of our country and government are now trying to persuade the community to believe that a war of race would result from giving the black man the same measure of justice and rights which the white men claim for themselves. This will be found to be a groundless fear. Our national danger will always result from unequal and partial laws.

Peter Cooper, Republican and founder of Cooper Union,
letter to President Johnson, 1866

State of the South

There are those who deserve liberty and peace. There are those who do not.

Douglas Cater, Confederate soldier,
on Confederates at large, June 24, 1864

Does the South deserve to be regenerated & lifted up into noble prosperity by the triumph of the North & the Nation?

Reverend Thomas Starr King

I want a common school system which shall not rest on the charity of the North. If Alabama doesn't set it up, we will, and send her the bill.

Wendell Phillips, abolitionist, 1865

There are no colored schools down in Surry County; they would kill anyone who would go down there and establish colored schools.

Reverend William Thornton, ex-slave,
of Surry County, Virginia, testimony before
the Joint Committee on Reconstruction, 1867

Thus began the period of "Reconstruction" which more properly should be called "Destruction"—for this law destroyed the homes and happiness of the South to an extent not cause even by the Federal armies in a hundred great battles.

Elizabeth Avery Meriwether, Memphis,
of the 1867 Reconstruction Acts

Do the Reconstruction acts of Congress propose to give us this peace? No— they give us war and anarchy, rather. They sow the seeds of discord in our midst.

Protest of convention of whites, September 21, 1867

Shall the white man be subordinate to the negro? Shall the property classes by robbed by the no property herd?

Montgomery *Daily Advertiser*, January 7, 1868

Thank God, the Southern oligarchy are blind. This stubbornness of the conquered to refuse the mild and generous terms offered by the conqueror, can only bring the latter to exact stronger guarantees . . . Their folly will save us and our liberties for the future. It is better for us that the work of reconstruction be protracted. Let the rebels do our work.

New Orleans Tribune, an African American newspaper,
on Southern states' rejection
of the Fourteenth Amendment, 1870

The wrongs for which our English ancestry brought the head of Charles the First to the block are trivial compared to these we now suffer.

The Natchez, Mississippi, *Democrat,*
on post-war taxation, December 8, 1874

Let him squirm. We mistake the tendency of affairs if real estate will ever get back to the happy condition it experienced in the good old Democratic days, when the "mud-sills" and "poor white trash" staggered under burdens of taxations that the ruling class might wallow in inglorious ease and increase in unearned wealth.

The Jackson *Weekly Pilot,* on the landowner
who complained of taxation, February 13, 1875

In short, North Carolina is now a white man's state and white men intend to govern it hereafter.

The Charlotte *Democrat,* on the victory
of the Democratic candidate for governor in 1876,
signaling the end of Reconstruction

The North and the South are simply convenient names for two distinct, hostile, and irreconcilable ideas . . . We tried to build up communities there which should be identical in thought, sentiment, growth and development, with those of the North. It was a FOOL'S ERRAND.

Character in Albion Tourgée's *A Fool's Errand*, 1879

We are very much pleased with the North, as well as we expected, & there is but one thing that mars, or one thing that is needed to make us happy now, as other things are working pretty well, that is, education, you know what is needed to take us along.

Martha Mortimer, African American, New York

"Now children, you don't think white people are any better than you because they have straight hair and white faces?"

"No, sir."

"No, they are no better, but they are different, they possess great power, they formed this great government, they control this vast country . . . Now what makes them different from you?"

"Money!"

"Yes, but what enabled them to obtain it? How did they get money?"

"Got it off us, stole it off we all!"

Miss Stanley, Northern schoolteacher, and her African
American pupils, in Kentucky after the war

Extending the Vote

The reconstruction of rebel states without Negro suffrage is a practical surrender to the Confederacy.

Wendell Phillips, abolitionist

If they were led to the polls, I think the act of voting with them would be a merely physical act.

Stephen Powers, reporter to the Cincinnati *Commercial*,
on Southern blacks, 1866

It is because they would not consent at the beginning to give civil rights to the negroes that the Southern states are now being forced to give them political rights. Years might have elapsed before the North decided to do complete justice to the black race, but the obstinacy of the slave holder forced it upon them.

Georges Clemenceau, correspondent to the Paris *Temps*,
on the Reconstruction Acts of 1867

Can you have the heart to ask colored men to vote for men who deny that they are capable of voting intelligently? Can you ask us to vote our liberties away forever?

"Address to the Native Whites,"
by a delegation of South Carolina blacks,
explaining why they were going to vote Republican in 1867

[I]n a government where the people are to be acknowledged sources of power, the duty of changing the laws and rulers by appeal to the ballot, and not by rebellion—should be taught to all children.

Horace Mann, founder of the Northern public school system

The slave of yesterday, who knew no law but the will of the master, is today to be invested with the control of the government.

Protest of convention of whites, September 21, 1867

Our "pathway" is straight to the ballot box, with no variableness nor shadow of turning . . . We demand in the Reconstruction suffrage for all the citizens of the Republic. I would not talk of Negroes or women, but of citizens.

Elizabeth Cady Stanton, letter, January 13, 1868

The enfranchised negroes, in general, exercised their new power quietly, considerately, and well—with far more regard for their old masters, and far less prejudice of race than could have been anticipated.

Reverend David Macrae, Scottish visitor to the South

I know the time will come when every man and woman in the country will have the right to vote. I acknowledge the superiority of women. There are large numbers of the sex who have an intelligence more than equal to our own. Is it right or just to deprive these intelligent beings of the privileges we enjoy?

William Whipper, delegate,
South Carolina Constitutional Convention, 1868

The right of citizens to vote shall not be denied or abridged by the United States or by any State on account of race, color, or previous condition of servitude.

The Fifteenth Amendment to the Constitution,
ratified March 30, 1870

Ku Klux Klan

The government builded schoolhouses, and the Ku Klux Klan went to work and burned 'em down. They'd go to jails and take the colored men out and knock their brains out and break their necks and throw 'em in the river.

Freed slave, on the Ku Klux Klan, formed in 1866

The way things are, we cannot vote. That's just the way it is. It's not worthwhile for a man to vote and run the risk of his life.

> Essic Harris, freed African American in North Carolina,
> on the Ku Klux Klan's reign of terror, 1868

The Klux is the living dead, and it is the strength of weakness.

> Edward H. Dixon, 1868

It is rapidly organizing wherever the insolent negro, the malignant white traitor to his race, and the infamous squatter are plotting to make the South utterly unfit for the residence of the decent white man.

> Edward Pollard, editor of the Richmond *Examiner*,
> of the Ku Klux Klan, 1868

I believe the object of the Klan is to whip unarmed negroes, scare timid white men, break up elections, and interfere with the State government and steal and plunder the goods of the people.

> Reverend H. O. Hoffman, Shelbyville, Tennessee, 1868

There is no intention or desire on the part of the civil authorities or the community at large to bring the murderers to justice. Those who could will not, and those who would are afraid.

> Joseph W. Gelray, inspector for the Freedmen's Bureau,
> report on the activities of the Ku Klux Klan
> in Tennessee, 1868

REV. MR. HOFFMAN: Your name is before the council. Heaven!! We will attend to you. You shall not call us "villains"—damn you.

> KU-KLUX, 1868

Bands of Ku-Klux prowl like wolves through the country for prey, and every week brings us tidings of some fresh work of midnight villainy.

African American schoolteacher in Alabama, 1870

There is no invasion which I am called upon to repel, and no insurrection which I am called upon to suppress.

Robert Scott, governor of South Carolina,
expressing a reluctance to act against the Ku Klux Klan, 1871

Forrest commanded more brave men in the invisible army than he did while in the Confederate army.

Member of the Ku Klux Klan,
speaking of Nathan Bedford Forrest,
former Confederate general and grand wizard
of the realm of Tennessee

Echoes

Reconstruction in Alabama was a tightly drawn struggle between Virtue, as represented by the Democrats, and Vice, as represented by the Republicans.

Horace Mann Bond, historian, describing the
"general notion" of Reconstruction, 1938

My father used to tell me that poverty and illiteracy in the South resulted from the way we were treated when the war was over, when they burned the schools down, burned the railroads, just desecrated the South.

George Wallace, former Alabama governor

The so-called radical Reconstruction of the Confederate South was the final bewildering act in the great drama of the American Civil War. It involved the startling elevation of a recently enslaved and still despised race, an attempt at the most radical redistribution of political power in the history of the nation, and an overwhelming and dreadful reaction well symbolized by the terrorism of the Ku Klux Klan.

Otto H. Olsen,
Reconstruction and Redemption in the South, 1980

Since the Negro has finally succeeded in penetrating the conscience of the best Whites, and since the worst Whites are muzzled by our need to grant the Negro his equality or sink a little faster into the icy bogs of the Cold War, the Negro knows he need merely ape the hypocrisies of the white bourgeoisie, and he will win. It is a partial misapprehension. In the act of concealing himself, the Negro does not hasten his victory so much as he deadens the taste of it.

Norman Mailer, *The Presidential Papers*, 1963

For a battle-call, rousing to arms if need be, years, centuries hence. —Walt Whitman, "Not the Pilot"

Veterans

Men dragged about with their regiments, some in the third week of fever, came in speechless or wandering and died just after getting on a clean bed. This was the "grand march home."

Jane Stuart Woolsey, Fairfax Seminary Hospital,
Alexandria, Virginia, on soldiers returning at the end of the war

As was to be expected, the returned soldiers are flooding the streets already, unable to find employment.

Fincher's Trade Review, June 1865

He brings his regiment home—
Not as they filed two years before,
But a remnant half-tattered, and battered, and worn,
Like castaway sailors, who—stunned
By the surf's loud roar,
Their mates dragged back and seen no more—
Again and again breast the surge,
And at last crawl, spent, to shore.

Herman Melville (1819–1891),
"The College Colonel"

There they were, the heroes of the army of Virginia, walking home, each with
his pass in his pocket, and nothing else. To run after them, to call them in, to
feel honored at shaking those rough hands, to spread the table for them, to
cry over them, and say again and again, "God Bless you all; we are just as
proud of you, and thank you just as much as if it had turned out differently";
this was a work which stirred our inmost souls.

Cornelia Spencer,
The Last Ninety Days of the War in North Carolina, 1866

They are treated worse than beggars. I issued rations to 78 men from Lee's
army passing through here—home—their own state, who had eaten nothing
for 48 hours; had been refused a bite to eat because they were ragged and dirty.

Alva Griest, Union soldier from Indiana,
on treatment of soldiers by the citizens
of Macon, Georgia, after the war

I agree with your condemnation of armchair pacifists on the general ground that
until the world has got farther along war not only is not absurd but is inevitable
and rational—although of course I would make great sacrifices to avoid one.

Oliver Wendell Holmes Jr., letter to Sir Frederick Pollock,
sentiments on war, having served with the Union army
at Antietam and Fredericksburg

No mortal man can Truth restore,
Or say where she is to be sought for.
I know what uniform I wore—
Oh, that I knew which side I fought for.

Ambrose Bierce (1842–1914),
"The Hesitating Veteran," a condemnation of attempts
to prevent blacks from having political rights

While my wife at my side lies slumbering, and the wars are over long,
And my head on the pillow rests at home, and the vacant midnight passes,
And through the stillness, through the dark, I hear, just hear, the breath of my
    infant,
There in the room as I wake from sleep this vision presses upon me;
The engagement opens there and then in fantasy unreal,
The skirmishers begin . . .

Walt Whitman (1819-1892), "The Artilleryman's Vision"

Fold it up carefully, lay it aside;
Tenderly touch it, look on it with pride;
For dear to our hearts must it be evermore,
The jacket of gray our loved soldier-boy wore.

Caroline Augusta Ball, "The Jacket of Gray"

Strangers kept filing through our house, kept not wiping their feet, come to
see the final vet of the War Betwixt States propped up. All them boys in blue
were cold in Yankee earth. Captain had tricked the winning side by holding
on the last, too proud to quit, maybe too cranky. Oh he was a sight—gray
uniform bunched over his pajamas, beard wild as a hedge and white to match
his cataracts grown big as ice cubes. Above the bed he'd hung a tintype of his
missing buddy, he kept a rusty musket within easy reach.

Allan Gurganus,
Oldest Living Confederate Widow Tells All

As the music swelled toward him, the entire past opened up on him out of nowhere and he felt his body riddled in a hundred places with sharp stabs of pain and he fell down, returning a curse for every hit . . . then a succession of places—Chickamauga, Shiloh, Marthasville—rushed at him as if the past were the only future now and he had to endure it.

Flannery O'Connor, "A Late Encounter with the Enemy,"
about a 104-year-old Confederate veteran

The tale is told. The sun shines brightly as before, the sky sparkles with the trembling stars that make the night beautiful, and the scene melts and gradually disappears forever.

Sam Watkins, Confederate private

Grand Review, Washington, D.C., May 1865   (Photographed by Matthew Brady)

Legacy of the War

The End of an Era

It has carried mourning to almost every home, until it can be almost said that the "heavens are hung in black."

Abraham Lincoln, on the Civil War

I see much of good resulting from war in its effects upon the character of our people. It will teach them to obey, if it lasts, & it will further teach them to reverence great men, a lesson long forgotten.

Thomas White, Boston, November 11, 1861

At least to pray—is left—is left / Oh Jesus—in the Air—I know not which
thy chamber is— / I'm knocking—everywhere— / Thou settest Earthquake in
the South— / And Maelstrom in the Sea— / Say, Jesus Christ of Nazareth— /
Hast thou no Arm for Me?

> Emily Dickinson, poet,
> after the battle of Antietam, late 1862

Making History

Nations can sufficiently live only as they find how to energetically die. In
this view, some of us have felt, for a long time, the want of a more historic life,
to make us a truly great people. This want is now supplied; for now, at last, we
may be said to have gotten a history.

> Horace Bushnell, transcendental minister,
> shortly after the end of the war

History deals with what is, and tis folly to discuss what might have been.

> William T. Sherman, Union general

Dear old Virginia! A birthplace is always dear, no matter under what circumstances you were born, since it revives in memory the golden hours of child-
hood. . . and the warm kiss of a mother.

> Elizabeth Keckley, African American returning to Virginia
> as a free woman and a member of the
> U.S. president's official touring party, April 1865

That our national democratic experiment, principle, and machinery could tri-
umphantly sustain such a shock, and that the Constitution could weather it,
like a ship a storm, and come out of it as sound and whole as before, is by far
the most signal proof yet of the stability of that experiment—Democracy—
and of those principles and that Constitution.

> Walt Whitman

Now that God has smitten slavery unto death, He has opened the way for the redemption and sanctification of our whole social system.

Edward Beecher, 1865

The great lesson which we have learned from the war, if we have learned any lesson at all, is that homogeneousness, social as well as political, is the first condition of our national existence.

E. L. Godkin, editorial in the *Nation*, September 21, 1865

Let us pray that the terrible historic tragedy of our time may not have been enacted without instructing our whole beloved country through pity and terror.

Herman Melville, 1866

The meaning of the war itself was never discussed enough for the children to realize it or understand it . . . we never heard much talk about Stuart, Johnston, Jackson or Lee. The war was over—and the new born generation was making a start at forgetting it.

Son of a Confederate veteran, Louisiania, born in 1872

Such was the war. It was not a quadrille in a ball-room. Its interior history will not only never be written—its practicality, minutiae of deeds and passions, will never even be suggested.

Walt Whitman

What the American public always wants is a tragedy with a happy ending.

William Dean Howells, in conversation with Edith Wharton

Echoes

[The Civil War] created in this country what had never existed before—a national consciousness. It was not the salvation of the Union; it was the rebirth of the Union.

Woodrow Wilson, U.S. president, Memorial Day 1915

The War meant that Americans saw America. The farm boy of Ohio, the trapper of Minnesota, and the pimp of the Mackerelville section of New York City saw Richmond and Mobile. They not only saw America, they saw each other, and together shot it out with some Scot of the Valley of Virginia or ducked hardware hurled by a Louisiana Jew who might be a lieutenant of artillery, CSA. By the War, not only Virginia and Louisiana were claimed for the union. Ohio and Minnesota were, in fact, claimed too.

Robert Penn Warren, *The Legacy of the Civil War*

Before 1861 the two words "United States" were generally rendered as a plural noun: the United States are a republic. The war marked a transition of the United States to a singular noun.

James M. McPherson, author, teacher, historian

There must be more historians of the civil war than there were generals fighting in it. Of the two groups, the historians are the more belligerent.

David Donald, author, historian

Grant, Sherman, Thomas, Lee, Johnston, Jackson, Hood, and all the rest gradually vanished like dinosaurs, but for a while they were giants that ruled the earth. In their prime, probably no armies as yet assembled could have matched them. Some lived on to see the age of airplanes, radios, skyscrapers, moving pictures, and world wars on an unimaginable scale, and when they were gone, their dust enriched the national trust.

Winston Groom, *Shrouds of Glory*, 1995

Bibliography

Alvarez, Joseph A. *From Reconstruction to Revolution: The Blacks' Struggle for Equality.* New York: Atheneum, 1971.

Berlin, Ira; Barbara J. Fields; Steven F. Miller; Joseph P. Reidy; and Leslie S. Rowland. *Free at Last: A Documentary History of Slavery, Freedom, and the Civil War.* New York: The New Press, 1992.

Blount, Roy, Jr., ed. Roy Blount's Book of Southern Humor. New York: W. W. Norton & Company, 1994. Boritt, Gabor S., ed. *Why the Civil War Came.* New York: Oxford University Press, 1996.

Carlisle, Henry, Jr. *American Satire in Prose and Verse.* New York: Random House, 1962.

Carter, Dan T. *The Politics of Rage.* New York: Simon & Schuster, 1995.

Cohodas, Nadine. *Strom Thurmond & the Politics of Southern Change.* New York: Simon & Schuster, 1993.

Connelly, Thomas L. *The Marble Man: Robert E. Lee and His Image in American Society.* New York: Alfred A. Knopf, 1977.

Culpepper, Marilyn Mayer. *Trials and Triumphs: The Women of the American Civil War.* East Lansing: Michigan State University Press, 1991.

Davis, Willam C. *A Government of Our Own: The Making of the Confederacy.* New York: Macmillan, 1994.

Delbanco, Andrew, ed. *The Portable Abraham Lincoln.* New York: Viking Penguin, 1992.

Eaton, Clement. *A History of the Southern Confederacy.* London: Collier Macmillan, 1954.

Faust, Drew Gilpin. *Mothers of Invention.* Chapel Hill, North Carolina: The University of North Carolina Press, 1996.

Fleming, Walter L., ed. *Documentary History of Reconstruction.* New York: McGraw-Hill, 1966.

Foner, Eric. *Reconstruction: America's Unfinished Revolution, 1863-1877.* New York: Harper & Row, Publishers, 1988.

Foner, Philip S. and Ronald L. Lewis, eds. *Black Workers: A Documentary History from Colonial Times to the Present.* Philadelphia: Temple University Press, 1989.

Harris, Leon A, ed. *The Fine Art of Political Wit.* New York: E. P. Dutton & Co., Inc., 1966.

Harwell, Richard B. *The Confederate Reader.* New York: Longmans, Green and Co., 1957.

Holzer, Harold, ed. *Dear Mr. Lincoln: Letters to the President.* New York: Addison Wesley, 1993.

Horwitz, Tony. *"A Death For Dixie." The New Yorker,* March 18, 1996.

Jordan, Ervin L. *Black Confederates and Afro-Yankees in Civil War Virginia.* Charlottesville, Virginia: University of Virginia, 1995.

Leckie, Robert. *None Died in Vain: The Saga of the American Civil War.* New York: HarperCollins, 1990.

Levine, Bruce. *Half Slave and Half Free: The Roots of the Civil War.* New York: Hill and Wang, 1992.

Lincoln, Abraham. *Speeches and Writings: 1859–1865.* New York: The Library of America, 1989.

Lowenfels, Walter, ed. *Walt Whitman's Civil War.* New York: Alfred A. Knopf: 1961.

McPherson, James M. *Battle Cry of Freedom.* New York: Oxford University Press, 1988.

_____. *The Negro's Civil War: How American Negroes Felt and Acted During the War for the Union.* New York: Pantheon, 1965.

Marius, Richard. *The Columbia Book of Civil War Poetry: From Whitman to Walcott.* New York: Columbia University Press, 1994.

Mitchell, Reid. *Civil War Soldiers: Their Expectation and Their Experiences.* New York: Viking, 1988.

Olsen, Otto H., ed. *Reconstruction and Redemption in the South.* Baton Rouge: Louisiana State University Press, 1980.

Ortiz, Victoria. *Sojourner Truth, A Self-Made Woman.* New York: HarperCollins Publishers, 1974.

The Oxford Dictionary of Quotations, 3rd edition. Oxford and New York: Oxford University Press, 1979.

Paludan, Phillip Shaw. *"A People's Contest": The Union and the Civil War, 1861–1865.* New York: Harper & Row, Publishers, 1988.

Perman, Michael. *The Road to Redemption: Southern Politics, 1869–1879.* Chapel Hill: The University of North Carolina Press, 1984.

Peterson, Merrill D. *Lincoln in American Memory.* New York: Oxford University Press, 1994.

Reeder, Russell Potter, Jr. *The Southern Generals.* New York: Duell, Sloan and Pearce, 1965.

Rose, Douglas. *The Emergence of David Duke and the Politics of Race.* Chapel Hill: University of North Carolina Press, 1992.

Royster, Charles. *The Destructive War: William Tecumseh Sherman, Stonewall Jackson, and the Americans.* New York: Alfred A. Knopf, 1991.

Rubing, Louis D., Jr., ed. *The American South: Portrait of a Culture.* Baton Rouge: Louisiana State University Press, 1980.

Silber, Irwin. *Songs of the Civil War.* London: Oxford University Press, 1960.

Smith, Page. *Trial by Fire: A People's History of the Civil War and Reconstruction.* New York: McGraw-Hill, 1982.

Straubing, Harold Elk. *Civil War: Eyewitness Reports.* Hamden, Conn.: Archon Books, 1985.

Wade, Wyn Craig. *The Fiery Cross: The Ku Klux Klan in America.* New York: Simon & Schuster, 1987.

Walton, Anthony. *Mississippi: An American Journey.* New York: Alfred A. Knopf, 1996.

Warren, Robert Penn. *The Civil War: Meditations on the Centennial.* New York: Random House, 1961.

Washington, James M., ed. *A Testament of Hope: The Essential Writings and Speeches of Martin Luther King, Jr.* New York: HarperCollins, 1986.

Wiley, Bell Irvin. *The Common Soldier in the Civil War.* New York: Grosset & Dunlap, 1952.

Wills, Gary. *Lincoln at Gettysburg: The Words that Remade America.* New York: Simon & Schuster, 1992.

Wilson, Edmund. *Patriotic Gore.* New York: Oxford University Press, 1962.

Zinn, Howard. *A People's History of the United States.* New York: Harper & Row, 1980.

Biographical Index

Subject Index